WINNING THE WAR OF WORDS

Essays on Zionism and Israel

EINAT WILF

Edited by
DANIEL RUBENSTEIN

Copyright © 2015 Einat Wilf
All rights reserved.
ISBN: 1515072975
ISBN 13: 9781515072973

"Years ago, when I suggested to the Knesset's Foreign Affairs and Defense Committee that Israel was facing a war based on words, ideas and images, and that it was a strategic threat, the veteran defense officials serving on the committee sent patronizing, avuncular glances my way. To those who have earned their stripes on the battlefield and in the war on terror, the notion that Israel could be threatened by words was ludicrous, and worse, feminine."

Israel Hayom
June 19, 2015

"This attack on the ideas that underpin Israel – the attack on its very legitimacy as a state – is taking place in a variety of forums, from international forums such as the UN and its various bodies, to courts, to academia, to the media, the NGO world and social networks. And so, with the failure of physical attacks, an intellectual attack is being mounted. While this attack does not appear at first to be dangerous and lethal as the others, it is no less threatening as it is targeting the very thing that makes Israel strong – its unique foundational idea…

EINAT WILF

While victory in this battle, as in others, is not likely to be swift, with the proper resources, organization, and determination it is within reach. After all, if there is any battle that the Jewish people should be able to win, it is the battle of words."

Presentation to International Consultation
of Jewish Parliamentarians
June 2011

ABOUT THE AUTHOR

Dr. Einat Wilf is a Senior Fellow with the Jewish People Policy Institute and the Baye Adjunct Fellow at the Washington Institute for Near East Policy. She was Chair of the Education, Sports and Culture Committee, Chair of the Knesset Sub-Committee for Israel and the Jewish People, and Member of the influential Foreign Affairs and Defense Committee in the 18th Knesset. Previously, Dr. Wilf served as Foreign Policy Advisor to Vice Prime Minister Shimon Peres and a strategic consultant with McKinsey & Company.

Dr. Wilf is the author of three books that explore key issues in Israeli society. Her first book, *My Israel, Our Generation*, is about Israel's past and future from the perspective of the younger generation. Her second book, *Back to Basics: How to Save Israeli Education (at No Additional Cost)*, offers a detailed and feasible policy proposal for improving Israel's education system. Her third and most recent book, *It's NOT the Electoral System, Stupid*, demonstrates through comparative analysis why Israel's electoral system is no worse than those of other democracies and therefore should not be changed.

Born and raised in Israel, Dr. Wilf served as an Intelligence Officer in the Israel Defense Forces. Dr. Wilf has a BA in Government and Fine Arts from Harvard University, an MBA from INSEAD in France, and a PhD in Political Science from the University of Cambridge.

TABLE OF CONTENTS

About the Author · v
**Chapter 1 The Dangerous Unraveling of
the Middle East** · 1
The New (Dis)Order of the Middle East · · · · · 3
The Battle between Old and New Loyalties · · 17
Minority Report: Jews Are the First Victims,
but Never the Last · 20
The Netanyahu Doctrine: *Si Vis Pacem,
Para Bellum* · 24
Regimes Value Their Survival More Than
Their Weapons · 27
Iran's Holocaust Denial: Flipping
the Finger to the West · · · · · · · · · · · · · · · · · 31
Israel: The Middle East's Neutral Bunker · · · 34

Chapter 2	**The International Community and**	
	The Limits of Good Intentions	**37**
	UNRWA: An Obstacle to Peace	39
	How Can Palestinians Be Refugees in	
	Their Own State?	46
	UN Security Council Proposals Damage	
	the Chances for Peace	50
	Well-Meaning Countries	
	Make Peace Less Likely	54
	Note to the United States:	
	We're Not Children	57
	Which Palestine is the UN in	
	Solidarity With?	61
	Palestinian Moves to Join ICC Have	
	Nothing to Do With Justice	66
Chapter 3	**A Vision For Peace**	**71**
	An Israeli Leftist Finds	
	a Glimmer of Hope	73
	Can Palestinians Accept the Existence of	
	a Jewish State – for Peace?	79
	Israelis Want Genuine Peace,	
	Not a Peace Process	82
	Towards a Zionism of Inclusion	85
Chapter 4	**Telling Our Story**	**105**
	The Search for a Single Zionist Story	107
	Zionism Denial	123
	President Obama's Lesson in Zionism	127

	What Does It Mean When We Say 'The Jewish State'? · · · · · · · · · · · · · · · · · · 131
	Israel at Sixty: Not for the Faint of Heart or Lazy of Mind · · · · · · · · · · · · · · · · 135
	An Israel Intellectual Defense Force · · · · · · 141
	A Roving Ambassador for Israel · · · · · · · · · 146
	Winning the Media War · · · · · · · · · · · · · · · 151
Chapter 5	**On Other Matters: Elections, Education, and Entitlement** · **155**
	It's Not the Electoral System, Stupid · · · · · · 157
	Back to Basics: How to Fix the Israeli Education System (at No Additional Cost) · · 173
	The Red Carpet Syndrome · · · · · · · · · · · · · 184

Chapter 1

THE DANGEROUS UNRAVELING OF THE MIDDLE EAST

"The Middle East as we've known it for the past one hundred years is unraveling right before our eyes. In its place, new and the old loyalties are raging a battle to shape the new Middle East. Any expectation that the battle between the old and new loyalties will be short, decisive and peaceful has nothing to rest upon. Any policy that ignores that is bound to fail."

The Telegraph
October 21, 2013

"Faced with events of such historic proportions and intense violence, the best prescription for Israel is to stay out – or more precisely, to be a 'neutral bunker.' Neutral in the sense that Israel should have nothing

EINAT WILF

to say regarding the events unfolding in the Arab world, and bunker in the sense that Israel's foreign and defense policy should operate with one goal: prevent the insanity gripping the Arab world from invading its borders."

Al Monitor
July 18, 2013

WINNING THE WAR OF WORDS

THE NEW (DIS)ORDER OF THE MIDDLE EAST

To understand the Middle East today and its future course, Europe of the 19th century provides some intriguing parallels. The shared characteristics of the two places and centuries shed light on the magnitude of transformation that the Arab world is undergoing. Reflecting on these parallels provides cause for both hope and fear.

Europe of the 19th century – or, more precisely, between the end of the Napoleonic Wars in 1815 and the breakout of World War I in 1914 – is frequently described as a continent and a century of peace, certainly in comparison to the horrific century that followed. But Europe of the 19th century was also a continent going through convulsions of transformation in fields ranging from technology and government to ideology and geopolitics. Like the mythical characters that change their appearance after having imbibed a magical drink, Europe jerked, agitated, stirred, and shook until it was transformed. No aspect of European life remained untouched by these convulsions. All that became great and all that turned horrific in Europe of the 20th century emerged during that era of transformation.

Europe of the 19th century experienced many rapid changes reminiscent of the Arab world today: technological innovation, and especially a revolution of mass-distributed, fast travelling information was undermining established hierarchies; advances in healthcare and science as well as changes in the economy led to rapid growth of the population; more people were living in cities and more of them were young. This combination of factors meant that information technology became the conduit of radical ideas challenging the established order, and the growing population of young people experiencing this rapid change was prepared to absorb these ideas and convey them further.

The ideas of Liberalism, Socialism, and Nationalism all vied to challenge the conservative order. They challenged the structure of government, the social contract, and the geopolitical structure. More people agitated for greater freedom, greater participation, greater representation, and greater expression of national identities. Driven in part by these ideas, the power architecture of Europe transformed as well. As demands for national expression and greater representation increased, the imperial order, at least on the continent, was challenged. Empires rose and fell, and new countries in the midst of Europe, such as Germany and Italy, coalesced around a national identity. Europe became a continent of several mid-sized powers – France, Britain, Germany, Russia, Italy, and Austria-Hungary – engaged in an ever-shifting web of alliances to protect interests and spheres of influence in the continent and abroad.

Those looking to relate the "Arab Spring" to the European "Spring of Nations" should have known that the European Spring, in its immediate aftermath, was a complete failure.

WINNING THE WAR OF WORDS

When the initial uprisings of peoples against their rulers in the Arab world were named the "Arab Spring," one of the clear historical references was the mold of the 1848 "Spring of Nations" that swept across peoples and nations in Europe and much of the world. The parallel seemed striking as the Arab Spring, much like the European one, was triggered by advances in information technology, by a rising and young population, and by ideas that inspired people to demand governments that were more representative, and societies that were more just. The phrase "Arab Spring" was intended to convey a sense of hope, and indeed for many months, hope was in the air.

However, those looking to relate the "Arab Spring" to the European "Spring of Nations" should have known that the European Spring, in its immediate aftermath, was a complete failure. The ideas of Socialism, Liberalism, and Nationalism represented such a profound challenge to the conservative order in Europe that there was virtually no room for gradual change or moderate accommodation. The only possible response was to quash these ideas – and those agitating for them – altogether.

The battle between the existing order and the emerging one was always going to be bloody, whether in Europe or the Middle East. As in the case of 19th century Europe, writing off the backlash of conservative forces was wrong and dangerous. When reactionary forces mobilized to quash the Arab Spring, many were quick to re-coin it "Arab Winter" and express disappointment at the rapid disappearance of hope for the immediate emergence of a liberal and democratic order. The European "Spring of Nations," no less than the Arab one however, was also rapidly quashed by a coalition of reactionary forces. Except for minor advances, such as the end of absolute monarchy in Denmark (the European Tunisia?), the conservative and authoritarian backlash was strong and swift, and erased much of the initial achievements of the rebelling peoples. The subsequent backlash was deeply violent with deaths reaching tens of thousands.

THE OTTOMAN SPRING OF NATIONS

One of the places that remained noticeably impervious to the broad sweep of the European "Spring of Nations," which reached as far as Brazil, was the Ottoman Empire. By the time the ideas of the "Spring of Nations" –from Liberalism to Arab nationalism– began to challenge the imperial order, it was late in the life of the Ottoman Empire, and World War I intervened to change its course. The demise of the Ottoman Empire therefore was not homegrown. It did not come about through the rising demands of its subject peoples for greater representation, democracy, and realization of national aspirations for self-determination. Rather it was the British and French empires – still unaware of their own imminent decline – that carved out the vast swathes of the Ottoman Empire in the course of World War I to create artificial states in the European mold. These artificially created states took little or no notice of the wishes of the governed – neither for representation and participation, nor for ethnic national cohesion – and the Ottoman Empire was forced to go through a sudden transformation that had nothing to do with the wishes of the people living in its midst.

The forced transformation of the Ottoman Empire from empire to artificial states shaped by external interests meant that for nearly a century the externally and arbitrarily drawn borders of the new states were held together by sheer force and, when available, legendary sums of oil money. The kings, put in place by the empires, and the authoritarian rulers who deposed them, had to forge new loyalties to King and Country that would erase the competing and powerful loyalties to tribe, religion, ethnic group, and nation. Nothing less than sheer brute force would be sufficient to secure the post-World War I order that shaped the modern Middle East.

But the "Spring of Nations" of 1848 ultimately did arrive in the lands previously under Ottoman control. In 2010, after a century and a half of delay, the areas of the Ottoman Empire got their own Spring. But the delayed "Ottoman Spring" meant that by the time the peoples rose, it was no longer against the Ottoman Empire, but against the artificially created states and regimes that were the outcomes of its forced carving. Like in 19th century Europe, the demands for more democratic government, for political reform, and for greater representation in the course of the Arab Spring were tied with the rise of sectarian sentiments and the demand to find proper political expression for those separate groups.

EINAT WILF

It is no accident that the top mid-sized regional powers which have not had a history of being subject to the Ottoman Empire – Turkey, Iran, and Israel – are those that enjoy the most distinct sense of national identity.

Once the century-old structures were exposed in their artificiality, the old identities that laid low for nearly a century rose to the surface to claim their due. In Europe, these were called "nations" and "peoples;" in the Middle East they are called "tribes," "sects," and "ethnicities" but the principle remains the same. Groups that claim cohesiveness based on history, language, culture, and kinship are rising up, demanding that political structures that do not give expression to these groupings – whether they are multiethnic empires, states artificially created by colonial forces, or small principalities – give way to new structures that better reflect the groups' demands for more cohesive political expression.

Just as the empires did not easily give way to the demands of the subject peoples for national expression, and just as Germany and Italy did not emerge from disparate principalities without bloody battles, it would be wrong to expect the post-World War I order in the Middle East to simply fade away in the face of the rising ancient identities. The identities created during the century between the breakup of the Ottoman Empire and the Arab Spring, despite being relatively new, cannot be written off easily. Current actors in the Middle East have grown up as Syrians, Iraqis, Jordanians, and Saudis, and that has power. These new identities also have the power of interests: powerful economic and military interests are tied to keeping the new identities alive, and they will not give in without a very bloody fight.

A NEW POWER ARCHITECTURE

Amidst this bloody fight, a new architecture of the Middle East can be glimpsed. As the Cold War's domination of the geopolitics of the Middle East recedes, a new architecture is emerging, reminiscent of that of Europe in the 19th century. It is an architecture of mid-sized powers engaging in ever shifting alliances and covert and overt struggles to expand and protect their spheres of influence. Like in 19th century Europe, there is a strong connection between countries vying for influence and the cohesiveness of their national, ethnic, sectarian, and religious identities.

It is no accident that the top mid-sized regional powers which have not had a history of being subject to the Ottoman Empire – Turkey, Iran, and Israel – are those that enjoy the most distinct sense of national identity. Turkey, for obvious reasons, already went through the difficult process of establishing itself as a country with a distinct identity. As the heir to the seat of the Ottoman Empire it is a natural regional power in the areas that were previously under imperial control. While there is still much to be done in terms of greater openness, democratization, and national expression for minorities, Turkey's regime and coherence are only marginally threatened by the delayed "Ottoman Spring." Turkey is therefore well placed to play the role of a regional power.

Iran was never part of the Ottoman Empire, and in addition to its distinct Islamic Shiite identity, it has a historical Persian identity that provides it cohesion and coherence. While its regime is highly vulnerable to the ideas of the "Arab Spring," its national identity is less so (even though there are minorities that might demand greater voice, such as the Azeris or the Kurds). Even if its regime were toppled, its borders and national coherence are likely to remain intact. Coupled with its vast resources and power, Iran is also well placed to play the role of a regional power. It has clear interests in expanding its sphere of influence, particularly when it comes to the Shiites of the Middle East.

Israel is the third non-Arab regional player in the region. Israel has been traditionally viewed as a foreign and colonial insert in the Middle East, an outcome of the colonial carving of the Ottoman Empire even more than countries such as Jordan, Iraq, and Syria. However, the historical connection between the Jewish people and their land points to a possible transformation of Israel and the story of Israel in the context of the "Arab Spring." In this new context, the perception of Israel in the Middle East might change from that of a colonial foreign insert to the national expression of the Jewish people, indigenous to the region. While the Jewish people began their struggle for national expression with the European "Spring of Nations," which is where they were located in the 19th century, given that their national aspirations were always directed to the Land of Israel, they are more properly thought of as a nation that arose to demand its self-determination in the Ottoman context.

There is no reason to accept any claim that the Arab Middle East is somehow impervious to the human desire for freedom and self-expression.

However, given that the "Spring of Nations" came to the lands of the Ottoman Empire more than a century and a half later, it is only now that the Jewish people can hope to become accepted as an indigenous people of lands of the Ottoman Empire. Their unique story can now be understood as straddling both the European Spring of Nations and the "Ottoman Spring." The idea of Jewish self-determination was born in Europe, but it could only be realized in their ancient homeland, an area previously under Ottoman control. The self-determination of the Jewish people then finally comes of age and could become accepted and locally integrated with the "Ottoman Spring."

Israel's democracy and power mean that it is not domestically vulnerable to the "Arab Spring," but the acceptance of Israel as a legitimate actor in the Middle East has been the greatest obstacle to its ability to be an integral, and certainly an overt, party to alliances in the region. If this negative perception changes, Israel might find itself openly accepted as a legitimate regional power.

While the top regional powers in the areas previously under Ottoman control are non-Arab, among those in the Arab world, Egypt and Saudi Arabia are the most substantial players. Egypt always enjoyed a distinct cohesive character, given its identity as a nation and people that date back to pre-Islamic times. Saudi Arabia, while an outcome of the artificial carving of the Ottoman Empire, always enjoyed heightened status as the historical seat of Arab identity. However, unlike Turkey, Iran, and Israel, the ideas and forces of the "Arab Spring" all present substantial challenges to the regimes of Egypt and Saudi Arabia. These regimes therefore need to invest far more of their efforts in preserving domestic stability, while also seeking to play a substantial regional role. Among the Arab countries, one could also consider Qatar, which, due to information technology and massive financial and natural resources, is able to punch above its weight as a regional player.

One more regional power worth mentioning is the new "Czarist" Russia. This is no longer the Soviet Union superpower player of the Cold War era. As the Cold War era architecture of the Middle East has receded and the Soviet Union disintegrated, Russia has returned to its traditional place as a regional actor in the Middle East. Russia is now again a mid-sized power protecting its regional interests, and seeking to expand and defend its sphere of influence in the area that is in its immediate vicinity.

All of these regional powers appear to be engaging, to one extent or another, in a web of shifting alliances, overt and covert, to protect their immediate interests and to prevent as much as possible any threats to the stability of their regimes. While these alliances have not yet coalesced into official treaties with memorable names such as "The Triple Alliance" and the "*Entente Cordiale*," they already seem to be playing traditional sphere-of-influence regional politics that would not shame the Europeans of the 19th century.

Torn between these regional players and within themselves are Syria and Iraq, and Libya, while other countries are in danger of being torn apart as well. The borders of these countries do not match those of the peoples within them and they are still in the throes of bloody battles between the old identities of sect, tribe, religion, ethnicity, as well as the new identities created in the wake of World War I.
    The European experience, especially with respect to Germany and Italy, demonstrates that the battles in Syria and Iraq could have a profound impact on reshaping the geopolitical architecture of the region, especially if coupled with extremist ideology. As the Shiite parts of Iraq are becoming part of the Iranian sphere of influence, and Iraqi Kurdistan establishes itself as a separate nation-state, could the Sunni parts of Iraq and Syria join together to truly become the "Islamic State of Iraq and Syria/Levant?" Should the goal of the Al Qaeda affiliated Islamist jihadists in Syria and Iraq to create an Islamic nation in the lands of Iraq and Syria/Levant be taken seriously? Could the Islamic State of Iraq and Syria/Levant, if established one day, be the Arab equivalent of Nazi

Germany? Could it be the newly formed state in the region's midst based on a radical and murderous ideology?

THE CASE FOR HOPE, THE CASE FOR FEAR

Parallels between different regions and across different centuries, by their very nature, are never precise. They are not predictive and may mean nothing, but as we seek to make sense of events of grand sweep, they inspire us to think of the possible implications of these momentous developments and their future course.

The hopeful message to emerge from the European experience is that ultimately the ideas that captured the imagination during the brief moment of the "Spring of Nations" triumphed. In the long run, the conservative backlash failed to quash the ideas that motivated the "Spring of Nations," which remained the most powerful ideas to determine the course of Europe up to the present era. The peoples of Europe ultimately did gain their freedom and establish democratically elected regimes that are representative of their peoples – including even women people. They created economic regimes that included public systems of health, education, welfare, and social security that the socialists of the 19th century would not have even dared imagine, and organized themselves into nations that recognize the aspirations of their distinct people, without giving up on the dream of a unified Europe. This is a triumph of the human spirit and the ability of ideas to shape a continent of freedom, prosperity, and peace.

WINNING THE WAR OF WORDS

There is no reason to accept any claim that the Arab Middle East is somehow impervious to the human desire for freedom and self-expression. The European experience demonstrates that even if reactionary forces have quashed initial revolts in the Middle East, this does not mean that ultimately the peoples of the region will not have their representative governments, or that the women of the Middle East will not one day be free and equal, or that Middle Eastern economies will not one day be open and competitive, or that societies will not be more fair. The peoples of the Middle East want these things no less than those of Europe in the 19th century, and the reactionary backlash does not mean that they want it any less. A future of freedom, prosperity, and peace is still very much a possibility for the future of the Middle East.

The Arab world is now wandering in its own desert, undergoing its own misery. If the transformation takes only forty years, we should all – peoples of the Middle East and the world – count ourselves lucky.

The disturbing and almost frightening message to emerge from the European experience is that the path to the realization of the noble ideas of human freedom and justice included two world wars, many regional wars, civil wars, massacres, genocide, Fascism, Nazism, Communism, dictatorships, and tyrannies that all had to be overcome and destroyed for human freedom and democracy to take hold. Many Europeans, enjoying their present state of peace, democracy, and prosperity forget the price that was paid on the path to the present. They expect other countries and regions to somehow smoothly transition from one condition to the next. But the lesson from the European experience is that the transitions from a conservative to a liberal order, from empires to nations, and from tyranny to freedom are never easy. They are bloody. They are vicious and they exact a heavy human toll. The more noble the ideas and the greater the aspirations, the more they challenge the existing order, and thus the greater the backlash they bring about.

Whether one chooses to take the hope or the fear from the European experience, if the path to the final breakup of the Ottoman Empire and the establishment of peace, prosperity, and democracy across the areas previously under its control are less bloody than such processes in the European case, it should be considered a miracle and a triumph of human action. As the Jewish people across the world celebrate in Passover their own story of transformation from slaves to free men, from imperial subjects to sovereign people, from individuals to nation, they also remember that this transformation took no less than forty years of misery and wandering in the desert. The Arab world is now wandering in its own desert, undergoing its own misery. If the transformation takes only forty years, we should all – peoples of the Middle East and the world– count ourselves lucky.

Turkish Policy Quarterly
Spring 2014

WINNING THE WAR OF WORDS

THE BATTLE BETWEEN OLD AND NEW LOYALTIES

The Middle East as we've known it for the past one hundred years is unraveling right before our eyes. In its place, new and the old loyalties are waging a battle to shape the new Middle East. Any expectation that the battle between the old and new loyalties will be short, decisive and peaceful has nothing to rest upon. Any policy that ignores that is bound to fail.

For nearly a century, the contours of the Middle East were put into place by World War I's victorious British and French empires. Their award: sharing the spoils of the dissolved Ottoman Empire. The lines drawn by Sykes and Picot in 1916 have become the borders of Turkey, Lebanon, Syria, Iraq, Saudi Arabia, and Jordan. For the next one hundred years, these externally and arbitrarily drawn borders were held together by sheer force and, when available, legendary sums of oil money. The kings, put in place by the empires, and the authoritarian rulers who deposed them, were able to forge together in the fires of war and oppression new loyalties to King and Country. Tens of millions of people were no longer Ottoman subjects of varying backgrounds. They were now proud Syrians, Iraqis, Libyans, and Jordanians.

This Middle East is gone with the sandstorm. The liberalizing forces of free information are undermining the power of authorities the world over. This, combined with the decreasing power of oil, the receding regional role of both former Cold War superpowers, and the apparent lessened

17

usefulness of Israel-hatred as a galvanizing tool, is blowing the top off this century old pressure cooker. Today, bubbling up to the surface are the old loyalties – ethnic, religious, sectarian, and tribal – that have laid low for nearly a century. This dirty mess, splattered across the walls of the old Middle East, is the new battle taking place today between old loyalties and new.

These new loyalties, despite their "newness," cannot be written off easily; the old loyalties, as old as they are, are far more powerful than our modern sensibilities would care to admit. The new loyalties have been around since the countries' establishment. Current actors in the Middle East have grown up as Syrians, Iraqis, Jordanians, and Saudis. That in itself has power. The new loyalties also have the power of interests: powerful economic and military interests are tied to keeping the new loyalties alive, and they will not give in without a very bloody fight. The fight will continue to be bloody, because the old loyalties are far more powerful than our notion of progress would concede. Ancient ethnic, religious, sectarian, and tribal loyalties cast a heavy shadow over people's sense of self and identities, and not just in the Middle East.

We can be hopeful that a new peaceful Middle East will one day emerge, but not before the old and new loyalties have spent themselves in prolonged and continuing butchery.

WINNING THE WAR OF WORDS

Not so long ago, Yugoslavia blew up in a murderous civil war when the pressure cooker of Tito's autocratic rule was lifted. Neighbors and family members slaughtered each other in the name of loyalties supposedly long forgotten. Modern Europeans who thought they had put their own ethnic and national butchery behind them, watched in horror how century-old loyalties and rivalries proved far more powerful than the modern Yugoslavian identity. And Yugoslavia was just the tail end of several centuries in which the European continent was engulfed in ongoing murderous battles between competing loyalties to kings and princes; nations and empires. The current impressive, modern, and peaceful structure of Europe could only emerge once the bloody battle between all the competing loyalties was spent.

It is too early, by decades and even centuries, to tell what new structure will emerge in the Middle East once the sand settles from the Arab Spring. This is not just a basic struggle for freedom and democracy against autocracy and Islam. Such thinking fails to give the ancient loyalties their due and ignores the numerous fissures that cut across the region. We can be hopeful that a new peaceful Middle East will one day emerge, but not before the old and new loyalties have spent themselves in prolonged and continuing butchery.

The Telegraph
October 21, 2013

MINORITY REPORT: JEWS ARE THE FIRST VICTIMS, BUT NEVER THE LAST

Just the other day, my Christian Lebanese colleague, whom I haven't seen in two years, sat down across from me at the lobby of a Washington DC hotel and said, "We miss you." As much as we are friends, he didn't mean "me" personally.

He elaborated, "We, the Arabs of the Middle East, miss you – the Jews." I smiled at the irony.

He went on to explain that while it has been more than sixty years since nearly a million Jews of the Arab Middle East were expelled and forced out of their home countries, it is now becoming evident that this merely foreshadowed things to come.

He recounted his horror by the rising tide of Islamic brutality, genocide, and ethnic cleansing of Christian communities that is taking place everywhere the Islamic State is gaining ground. Just like the Jewish communities, those Christian communities – gone overnight – were there before the birth of Islam and the Arab conquest of the region.

He said that he is terrified to think of an Arab Middle East without minorities. He expressed fear that the intolerance demonstrated towards the Jews decades ago is now being turned towards almost all other minorities from Christians to Alawites to Shiites to the Sunni Muslims who fail to uphold the demented standards for Muslim piety set by the Islamic State.

My Arab colleague was brave enough to admit this simple truth that the world has learned over and over again, and yet seems to never internalize: It starts with the Jews. It never ends with the Jews.

Rising tides of hatred, intolerance, and brutality are not satisfied once they have rid society of its Jews. Sooner or later, others will follow. Not only does it never end with the Jews. It is never really about the Jews. That is why it never ends with them. Hatred of Jews is about those who hate – not about those who are hated.

When the "Jewish Question" was discussed in Europe of the 19th century, it was not really the Jewish Question – rather it was the European Question. It was about what Europe is and what it wants to be.

Tragically, Europe worked out its identity as a continent, its ideologies, and its loyalties, on the back and ultimately, on the ashes, of the Jews, nearly destroying the entire European civilization in the process.

Rising tides of hatred, intolerance and brutality are not satisfied once they have rid society of its Jews. Sooner or later, others will follow.

When Europe is experiencing yet again rising tides of hatred and intolerance towards Jews – whatever else it might call it and however it might seek to mask it – it is time for Europe to ask what is wrong with Europe and not what is wrong with the Jews. Europe's vision of itself is challenged from within and without, and this time around, it seems that many Jews don't plan to stick around to find out how Europe will resolve the European Question "this time around."

The Arab world is no different with respect to the "Jewish Question." It is not about the Jews, and not even about Israel and Zionism, it is about the question of Arab and Muslim identity. And, like Europe before it and, sadly perhaps still today, it is working out its identity, ideologies, and loyalties – initially on the back of the Jews and now on the back of other minorities.

The Christians of the Middle East believed they would find their peace and security by aligning themselves with Arab nationalism and becoming some of its most vocal defenders. They thought that by aligning themselves with Arab intolerance towards Jews, they would shield themselves from the simple fact that the vast majority of Arabs were Muslims and that as far as Muslim theology is concerned Christians, like Jews, are not and cannot be considered equal to Muslims.

With the advancing terror, my colleague expressed his desired to see the Jews back in Beirut, Alexandria, Baghdad, Damascus, Aleppo, Tripoli, and Casablanca, as they were for over a thousand years.

He believed that if the Jews were to return, the minorities of the Middle East could join hands together to promote a vision of pluralism and tolerance that would stem the tide of rising intolerance and brutality.

WINNING THE WAR OF WORDS

My colleague overlooked the irony that the only place in the Middle East where Christians were not fleeing, but were secure, growing, and prospering, was in the Jewish State of Israel.

Someday, perhaps, the Jews will return. Someday, perhaps, there will once again be bustling Jewish communities across the Arab Middle East.

Someday, perhaps, the Jews of Europe will reverse their renewed Exodus. Someday, these places might truly offer havens of peace, pluralism, and tolerance, and would settle the questions of identity that plague them.

Until that day – thank goodness for the Jewish state.

Irish Examiner
November 28, 2014

THE NETANYAHU DOCTRINE: *SI VIS PACEM, PARA BELLUM*

When Israeli Prime Minister Benjamin Netanyahu emerged from his meeting on Monday with President Barack Obama, he may have recognized in the president a fellow proponent of the Netanyahu Doctrine: to avoid the use of force, be ready to use it. After all, Obama had just reiterated that he won't take any options off the table on Iran, "including military."

Of course, the Netanyahu Doctrine is nothing new – the ancient Romans described it as *si vis pacem, para bellum*, "he who wants peace must prepare for war." Hebrew wisdom extolled self-restraint as the highest form of heroism, and such ancient wisdom has also guided Netanyahu's policies, and not only on Iran. But while this doctrine did not originate with Netanyahu, the prime minister has become closely associated with its application in the region, despite facing significant criticism.

The doctrine is simple to formulate, yet nearly impossible to successfully implement because to be a success, three components must be in place: the capability to use force, projection of a true willingness to use it, and a deep desire to avoid doing so. No one, including the leader, knows what will actually happen at the critical moment of decision regarding the use of force, but the other side should be sufficiently concerned and unsure to consider the threat credible. When done right, the doctrine is a masterful tightrope walk over the twin abyss of Vietnam and Munich: Prepare for war too much and you risk instigating the very war you wish to avoid; prepare too little and you risk encouraging aggression through weakness and appeasement.

But the artful balancing act needed to reach a successful diplomatic outcome means this approach can be easily misunderstood. Some mistake it for bluster, others for bluff. But it is neither. Building the capacity to use force and conveying the willingness to use it can easily lead outsiders to mistakenly interpret such acts as the policies of reckless leaders itching for war. These were precisely the accusations leveled at both Netanyahu and former Defense Minister Ehud Barak by retired Israeli security officials, who rang the alarm bells convinced they could save the country from "trigger happy cowboys."

Former Prime Minister Ehud Olmert, for example, has publicly hit out at Netanyahu and Barak for spending three billion dollars on "adventurous fantasies" and "military delusions" for operations that "will never be carried out." Yet such investment serves not only to build the capability to use force, but also conveys a willingness to use it. The same is true for the massive recruitment of reserves, who stood ready to enter the Gaza Strip during operation Pillar of Defense, but who never had to because diplomacy allowed the desired outcome of relative calm.

When done right, the doctrine is a masterful tightrope walk over the twin abyss of Vietnam and Munich: Prepare for war too much and you risk instigating the very war you wish to avoid; prepare too little and you risk encouraging aggression through weakness and appeasement.

When Netanyahu gave his now famous speech at the United Nations a year ago, memorably charting a red line to Iran's weapons nuclear program, many interpreted the speech as an Israeli attempt to entangle the United States in a war that would serve Israel's interest. But Netanyahu's goal was precisely the opposite. His speech was not about how to go to war – it was about how to avoid it. Netanyahu's message for the international community, and especially to the United States and its allies, was that a clear red line to Iran, backed by a credible military threat, was necessary for diplomacy to work.

The fact is that diplomacy alone was not going to achieve the aim of curbing Iran's nuclear ambitions. Diplomacy backed by force had a fighting chance. A year later, the results of Iran's elections and its recent "charm offensive" and offers of negotiations have proven this doctrine correct.

It is no accident that Netanyahu is at once considered Israel's most hawkish prime minister and yet has not actually taken the country to war.*[1] It is no accident that under his watch the number of Jews and Arabs killed as a result of violent conflict between has fallen noticeably. Too many make the mistake of judging Netanyahu by his hawkish rhetoric, and too few by the outcomes of his policies.

When implemented well, the outcome of the Netanyahu doctrine is peace, not war.

CNN
October 1, 2013

---

1 This sentence was written during an extended and rare period of calm before the Gaza war in the summer of 2014. To reconcile the Netanyahu Doctrine with that war, see "Netanyahu, the reluctant warrior" by Alan Dershowitz in the July 20, 2014, edition of *Haaretz*.

REGIMES VALUE THEIR SURVIVAL MORE THAN THEIR WEAPONS

Now that the deal to dismantle Syria's chemical weapons is nearly fully implemented, and the deal to slow down Iran's nuclear program is underway, it should be noted that both those deals were never about controlling the use and spread of weapons of mass destruction, but rather about preserving the regimes that would use them. The Assad regime in Syria and the Ayatollah regime in Iran both came to the respective negotiations tables with one goal in mind: preserve their regimes. The chemical weapons in Syria and the nuclear program in Iran only mattered to the extent they could contribute to preserving their regime.

When Assad the elder amassed a significant stockpile of chemical weapons, he was concerned about a variety of potential threats to his regime. He, as well as his son, was never under any illusions about the stability and legitimacy of the regime. As rulers of an artificially-created state, ruled by a ten percent Alawite minority, which is considered heretical by almost all Muslims, they knew they had to rely on brute force, repression, and butchery (in which the son has outdone father), to secure their rule and the privileges of their sect. The chemical weapons were a means to that end.

Then, as a result of a haphazard chain of events, Assad the younger faced the danger that his rule would be destabilized by an outside-led American intervention, just as he seemed to be gaining ground against the opposition forces. When he was given the option of averting this intervention by getting rid of the stockpile of chemical weapons under his control he faced no real dilemma. If his regime could be secured by ridding the country of chemical weapons, then the weapons were to prove themselves useful, as intended, for securing the regime, but in neutralizing, rather than using them.

Assad, with an astute sense for power and survival, understood what the West refuses to admit, that once the chemical weapons were gotten rid of, he would be free to continue his butchery and the threat to his regime would be lifted.

Those who were skeptical that Assad the younger would keep his side of the agreement failed to understand his end goal: Assad, with an astute sense for power and survival, understood what the West refuses to admit, that once the chemical weapons were gotten rid of, he would be free to continue his butchery and the threat to his regime would be lifted. Indeed, as it became clear that Assad was as serious about getting rid of the weapons as his father was about getting them – both for the same purpose of securing their regime – he (and his country) were left alone.

On this point, the Ayatollah regime of Iran is no different. The regime entered serious negotiations with the West this month regarding its nuclear program with the same goal of self-preservation. The Islamic republic is skating on thin ice, even if a little thicker than the Assad regime. It has already brutally quashed the green revolution and has been reaching the limits of brutal repression as an effective means of regime preservation. While the regime in Tehran might want to look to North Korea as a model of deceiving the West on its nuclear program, the people of Iran cannot endure the kind of repression that the North Korean dictator has wrought on his people.

The Ayatollahs in Tehran understand that they need to seek other models of survival. In doing so, they look towards the Soviet Union as what to avoid, and to China as what can be achieved. The Soviet Union, from this regime's perspective, introduced too much openness, which caused the USSR to quickly collapse. China, after Tiananmen, was able to introduce a slow, controlled form of economic openness, combined with continued social repression that preserved intact the rule of the Communist Party. For the Ayatollah regime following the Chinese path to regime preservation, means that it desperately needs sanction relief and the ability to gradually open up its economy to trade.

To preserve their regime, the Ayatollahs might be willing to go far, probably much further than anyone among the negotiators believes – this being the point that Prime Minister Netanyahu insists upon. What the West fails to understand in the Iranian case is that the nuclear program is only valuable to the extent that it helps secure the regime, and if due to the strict sanctions regime which prevents the pursuit of gradual economic openness as a means of regime preservation, it becomes less of an asset, it could conceivably be traded away. Indeed, if the regime felt that the economic pressure and the credible threat of military intervention were to threaten its very survival, it might, just as Assad did with the chemical weapons, go as far as give up the entire nuclear program altogether.

The Assad and Ayatollah regimes might be cruel, brutal, messianic, repressive, and bloody, but when it comes to their own survival, they make rational calculations. As the West embarks on negotiations for a permanent agreement with the Ayatollah regime, it must not lose sight of this very basic idea: what's at stake in the negotiations for the regime is its very survival, not its nukes.

Times of Israel
December 8, 2013

IRAN'S HOLOCAUST DENIAL: FLIPPING THE FINGER TO THE WEST

Iranian President Mahmoud Ahmadinejad has taken advantage yet again of the annual convening of the United Nations General Assembly to continue his proud tradition of Holocaust denial. One could safely assume that the intense interest that he shows in denying the Holocaust does not emerge from a passion for World War II history, and that the quest for historical truth is not what keeps him awake at night.

As Israelis, we interpret Holocaust denial as a direct attack on what some believe is the basis for Israel's legitimacy – a problematic claim that tends to marginalize the legitimacy of Zionism as an independence movement of Jewish self-determination. But there is a broader aspect at play: like a child finding a shiny toy, the Iranian president discovered at one point that along with the development of nuclear weapons, Holocaust denial was one of the fastest and most effective means – if not the most effective – of positioning himself as the leader of the axis of countries that challenge the West.

Since the 1990s, Holocaust remembrance has become universalized and went from a "Jewish issue" to a "humanity issue," especially in the West. Holocaust museums have been built around the world typically emphasizing the local and global contexts, rather than the Jewish one. One need only visit the Holocaust Museum in Washington's DC Mall, a symbol of everything American, and to embark on a viewing journey that begins with the images and voices of American soldiers who liberated the camps and ends on the shores of the United States and the Statue of Liberty, to witness a very different type of Holocaust remembrance narrative than the one of devastation and renewal with which we are familiar in Israel.

This process of universalizing Holocaust remembrance was aided by popular culture, especially in books and film, and through numerous countries' internal investigations in the wake of archives opening and high-profile struggles for restoration of property and compensation to survivors. This has led to many countries adopting Holocaust remembrance as a value in itself. This process reached its peak with the United Nations General Assembly resolution of November 2005 that set January 27th as International Holocaust Remembrance Day. The decision was welcomed in Israel, albeit accompanied by a sense of unease that "our" Holocaust is no longer just "ours." In this manner, Holocaust remembrance has become one of the most important markers of universal enlightenment and a shorthand for a whole set of values such as human rights, freedom, equality, and the dignity of man, and in so doing, has moved away from the particular Jewish context to become a signifier of belonging to a certain group – mostly that of the West.

In the era after the fall of Communism, Holocaust denial has become a symbol of extreme ideological opposition to the West. If in the process, one could also undermine Israel's legitimacy – that's just a bonus.

WINNING THE WAR OF WORDS

As Holocaust remembrance became identified with a certain set of values, so has Holocaust denial become a simple and effective means of flipping the finger to the Western world. In the era after the fall of Communism, Holocaust denial has become a symbol of extreme ideological opposition to the West. It's a particularly effective shortcut – no need to laboriously write a revolutionary manifesto and present an ideological alternative. It is enough to convene a Holocaust Denial conference and to gain immediate status as the "top dog" mounting the challenge to the West. If in the process, one could also undermine Israel's legitimacy – that's just a bonus.

Iran operates on several fronts to defy Western dominance, especially in the Middle East. Ahmadinejad's persistent and provocative Holocaust denial is not simply the ranting of a madman, but a conscious and planned element in this on-going challenge.

Jerusalem Post
September 28, 2009

EINAT WILF

ISRAEL: THE MIDDLE EAST'S NEUTRAL BUNKER

For more than two years, Israel has found itself in the eye of a storm. This is not to say that Israel has been at the center of events. Quite the contrary – the eye of the storm is a very quiet place. Israel has been eerily quiet. As Israelis look left and right, north and south, east and west, all they see is a tornado of chaos, massacres, instability, political and economic collapse, sectarian violence, gang rapes, religious fanaticism and civil wars. Yet, miraculously, amidst all this, Israel is stable, calm, democratic and prosperous.

The Post-World War I Order that shaped the Middle East for the past century is unraveling violently. The dark forces of hatred between sects, tribes, religions and classes that had been suppressed by sultans, kings and dictators have risen to the surface. If history is any guide, it will be decades or even centuries before these forces play themselves out. And if the French revolution is anything to go by, Egypt will see the high ideals of the initial days of its revolution realized in a century or two – not earlier.

There is tremendous hope in the desire expressed by people throughout the region for freedom and democracy, but even under the best of circumstances, the transition to stable, liberal democracy takes several decades, and the Arab world has nothing even approximating the best of circumstances. The combination of the democratic deficit, collapsing economies, corruption, illiteracy and poverty is the worst possible one.

Faced with events of such historic proportions and intense violence, the best prescription for Israel is to stay out – or more precisely, to be a "neutral bunker." Neutral in the sense that Israel should have nothing to say regarding the events unfolding in the Arab world, and bunker in the sense that Israel's foreign and defense policy should operate with one goal: prevent the insanity gripping the Arab world from invading its borders.

Faced with events in the Middle East of such historic proportions and intense violence, the best prescription for Israel is to stay out.

In the Middle East, Israel should aspire to emulate the model of Swiss neutrality. It should take no sides and express no preference whatsoever for one over another. Israel should have nothing to say for or against Syrian President Bashar al-Assad or Egypt's ousted president Mohammed Morsi or even hint at taking sides between Shiites and Sunnis. Israel should not try to employ the logic of "the enemy of the enemy is my friend" because in the Middle East, Israel is the exception – always the enemy. Any expression of preference by Israel will only serve to draw undesired attention to it and to discredit the side it supports.

This is not to say that Israel should not have an opinion on the desired outcome for the Arab world. The best possible outcome for Israel is the establishment of stable liberal democracies across the Middle East. Israel desires nothing more than to lose its status as the only one in the Middle East, and gain that of being the first of many.

But until this happy outcome is realized, Israel should prepare for decades in which its best policy will be to bunker down. Israel does not enjoy the benefit of the formidable Alps, and yet it should seek to emulate the Swiss not just in their neutrality, but also in the bunker mentality they were able to maintain for centuries. Switzerland managed to survive and prosper as a "neutral bunker" while Europe was torn apart by religious, sectarian, civil, national and world wars. For a long time to come, the Arab world will be as turbulent and violent as Europe was for most of its history. Israel's best hope for the future is to maintain neutrality throughout this time. The Israel Defense Forces and our political leadership have no more important priority.

Al Monitor
July 18, 2013

Chapter 2

THE INTERNATIONAL COMMUNITY AND THE LIMITS OF GOOD INTENTIONS

"The Palestinians don't need another UN Security Council resolution to achieve statehood in the West Bank and Gaza Strip. They could have it today by making peace with Israel."

The Sydney Morning Herald
February 15, 2015

"If Western countries truly want to remove obstacles on the road to peace, they cannot condemn the growth of settlements on one hand and condone the manufactured growth of the number of refugees on the other. Either both the growth of settlements and the inflation in the number of refugees should be treated as obstacles to peace, or neither should be."

Fathom
Autumn 2013

"Both Israelis and Palestinians are also very much aware of the decisions they need to make if they are to come to a full and complete peace agreement, one that recognizes the right of both peoples to the land. If they don't make those decisions, it's not because they don't know what they are."

CNN
May 1, 2014

UNRWA: AN OBSTACLE TO PEACE

One of the greatest obstacles to peace, and certainly the least acknowledged, is the perpetuation of the Palestinian refugee problem and the inflation of its scale by the United Nations Relief and Works Agency (UNRWA). Whereas the actual number of Arabs who could still claim to be refugees as a result of the Arab-Israeli war of 1947-1949 is today no more than several tens of thousands, the number of those registered as refugees is reaching 5 million, with millions more claiming to have that status.

THE UNRWA PROBLEM

Since the Second World War, the UN High Commissioner for Refugees has been responsible for the welfare of all refugees in the world and has assisted in their resettlement and relocation – so that nearly all of them are no longer refugees – with one exception: the Arabs from Palestine. By contrast, UNRWA, the organisation created specifically to handle the Arab refugees from Palestine from the 1947-1949 Arab-Israel war, has collaborated with the Arab refusal to resettle the refugees in the areas where they reside, or to relocate them to third countries. Worse, UNRWA has ensured that the refugee issue only grows larger by automatically registering descendants of the original refugees from the war as refugees themselves in perpetuity, for Palestinians, uniquely, refugeeness is an hereditary trait.

For several decades UNRWA has been engaging in an act of bureaucratic self-aggrandisement, inflating the numbers of those in its care, ensuring the growth of its budget. If the descendants of the Arab refugees from the Arab-Israeli war were treated like all other refugees, including the Jewish ones, they would not qualify for refugee status because almost all of them (upward of 80 per cent) are either citizens of a third country, such as Jordan, or they live in the places where they were born and expect to have a future such as Gaza and the West Bank. The Palestinians born in the West Bank and Gaza are not fleeing war and are not seeking refuge. They are considered citizens of Palestine by the Palestinian Authority itself, just like all other Palestinians born in these territories. No other people in the world are registered as refugees while being citizens of another country or territory. Moreover, if the European Union has adopted the policy that Gaza and the West Bank are territories to be allocated to Palestine – and some EU countries already recognise Palestine as a state – then it makes no sense for it to argue that people who were born and are living in Palestine are refugees from... Palestine.

The remaining 20 per cent of the descendants who are not Jordanian citizens or citizens of the Palestinian Authority in Gaza and the West Bank, are inhabitants of Syria and Lebanon who are by law denied the right to citizenship granted to all other Syrians and Lebanese. Yet, UNRWA does nothing to fight for the right of these Lebanese and Syrian-born Arabs to citizenship, collaborating in their discrimination and the perpetuation of their refugee status.

WINNING THE WAR OF WORDS

Why does this matter for peace? Because if millions of Arabs who are citizens of Jordan and the Palestinian Authority, or inhabitants of Syria and Lebanon, claim to be refugees from what is today Israel, even though they were never born there and never lived there, and demand that as a result of this refugee status they be given the right to relocate to Israel ('the right of return'), then the whole basis for peace by means of two states for two people crumbles. If Israel with its 6 million Jews and more than 1.5 million Arabs has to absorb between 5 and 8 million Palestinians then the Jews will be relegated again to living as a minority among those who do not view them as equals; the only country in which the Jews are a majority and can exercise their right to self-determination would be no more.

WESTERN COMPLICITY

Even more absurd is that UNRWA is funded by countries who support two states for two peoples. The United States, the EU, Canada, Japan and Australia fund 99 per cent of UNRWA's annual budget of over $1 billion, whereas the 56 Islamic countries who supposedly grieve for their Palestinian brethren supply only a few million dollars.

If the policy of Western countries towards the Jewish settlements in the West Bank were to take its cue from their policy towards the Palestinian refugees as shaped by UNRWA, it would go as follows: 'Go ahead Israel, build as many settlements as you want and keep expanding them in perpetuity. We will accept the settlements as a natural expansion of Israel. We will even support the expansion effort financially. Don't tell the settlers that they will ever need to leave their homes, teach them that it is their legal right to be there. We trust that when the day comes to negotiate peace with the Arab world you will do so in good faith and in a way that guarantees the existence of a sovereign and contiguous Arab state in Gaza and the West Bank.'

The welfare, education and health services provided by UNRWA could continue and even be expanded, but their provision should be based on need, not refugee status.

As it stands right now the policy of Western countries towards UNRWA is precisely that – it is essentially telling the Arab world: 'Go ahead and keep inflating the numbers of refugees in perpetuity by registering descendants of refugees as refugees themselves. Register them as refugees from Palestine even though they were born and are living in the Palestinian Authority. Allow them to maintain both a refugee status and citizenship from a third country. Keep telling them that even though they were born in Gaza and Ramallah, they are actually from Ashdod and Ashkelon and can realistically expect to live there soon. Keep them in a discriminated-against state in Syria and Lebanon, where their basic human rights are denied, just so they can keep the conflict alive. We trust that when the day comes to negotiate a final settlement with Israel, you will do so in good faith in a way that guarantees the coherence and existence of a Jewish state.'

If the first policy appears preposterous to Western governments who support peace by means of a two-state solution, then so should the second. If Western countries truly want to remove obstacles on the road to peace, they cannot condemn the growth of settlements on one hand and condone the manufactured growth of the number of refugees on the other. Either both the growth of settlements and the inflation in the number of refugees should be treated as obstacles to peace, or neither should be. Moreover, whereas Israel has demonstrated time and again that for peace with Egypt – and for much less than peace in Gaza and the northern West Bank – it will ruthlessly and effectively uproot settlements, the Palestinians have yet to demonstrate that they are willing to take even the smallest steps to give the refugee issue its true and proper proportions.

ALTERNATIVES

If the West truly wants to promote a coherent policy that supports a two-state solution and does not favour one side over another, it should use its power as the financial supporter of UNRWA to steer its practices along a more constructive path. The welfare, education and health services provided by UNRWA could continue and even be expanded, but their provision should be based on need, not refugee status.

If the EU wants its recent stringent steps against Israeli settlements to be taken as genuine efforts to keep the two-state solution alive as the path to peace, it must pursue policies that address all obstacles to peace.

In Gaza, where there is no Israeli presence and which is clearly part of Palestine, the continued registration of Palestinians living in Palestine as refugees should be discontinued. In the West Bank, in the areas under Palestinian Authority control, the funds currently going to UNRWA should go to the Palestinian Authority for the provision of services, while the designation of the citizens of the Palestinian Authority as refugees should also be discontinued. Finally, outside the West Bank and Gaza, UNRWA's work should be merged with that of the UN High Commissioner for Refugees and operate on the same basis as all other refugees in the world, with efforts directed at securing the equal rights of the descendants in Lebanon and Syria, where they were born and have lived their entire lives.

A first effort in this direction was taken in 2012 when the US Senate, acting on the initiative of Senator Mark Kirk, introduced an amendment to the budget bill, requesting that UNRWA report 'on the number of refugees that it services separate from their descendants.' The US Senate Appropriations Committee asked for nothing more than information and transparency in reporting in return for the 250 million dollars of US taxpayers' money that it supplies UNRWA annually. It did not ask for aid to be cut. It did not call for cessation of services to the millions of descendants; it only asked for transparency in numbers. Even though the amendment did not go through, given that the budget bill as a whole did not move forward, the US Senate sent out a powerful message for peace in that the attainment of a two-state solution cannot be congruent with UNRWA's practice of inflating the number of refugees. And if the EU wants its recent stringent steps against Israeli settlements to be taken as genuine efforts to keep the two-state solution alive as the path to peace, it must pursue policies that address all obstacles to peace.

Fathom
Autumn 2013

EINAT WILF

HOW CAN PALESTINIANS BE REFUGEES IN THEIR OWN STATE?

Sweden may not know it yet, but its recent recognition of the State of Palestine may conflict with its support for a United Nations Refugee organization that it backs to the tune of tens of millions of dollars per year.

Stockholm's October 30 recognition of the State of Palestine prompted Israel to withdraw its ambassador. Jerusalem insisted that supporting Palestinian unilateral moves at the United Nations will only make it more difficult to bring the Palestinians back to the negotiating table to iron out the thorny issues that have made peace so elusive. But the Swedes insisted that their recognition of Palestine was intended to promote the cause of "peaceful co-existence between Israel and Palestine."

That may sound well-intentioned, but here's the rub: Sweden is the fifth largest supporter of UNRWA – the United Nations Relief and Works Agency, which provides social and welfare services to the original Palestinian refugees from the 1947-1949 Arab–Jewish war.

UNRWA took quite a bit of heat for a Hamas tunnel found beneath one of its facilities during the Gaza war this summer, and for turning over rockets found at one of its facilities to Hamas "authorities." But that pales in comparison to the scorn it has earned for its policy of recognizing the descendants of the original refugees – a policy that has led to the mushrooming of refugee figures from 800,000 in 1949 to more than 5 million today.

Indeed, UNRWA has effectively perpetuated the refugee problem, making any amelioration or resolution of their situation that does not involve the demand to "return to Palestine" virtually impossible.

For the Swedes, the problem is not only that they supported this problematic arm of the UN to the tune of $54.4 million last year. Stockholm appears to have tied itself into a policy knot through its recognition of Palestine.

An estimated two million Palestinian refugees currently live in the West Bank and Gaza – the territory that Sweden recognizes as the State of Palestine. How can they continue to be registered as "refugees from Palestine" – the country to which they demand to return – if such a state already exists?

The Swedes say Palestine "fulfills the... criteria of international law: there is a territory, a people and a government."

The territory they refer to is defined by the pre-1967 cease-fire lines – meaning the West Bank and Gaza.

An estimated two million Palestinian refugees currently live in the West Bank and Gaza – the territory that Sweden recognizes as the State of Palestine.

How can they continue to be registered as "refugees from Palestine" – the country to which they demand to return – if such a state already exists? Sweden, in other words, has inadvertently exposed a fundamental contradiction in the policies of those who support UNRWA and also back the unilateral Palestinian statehood initiative. Indeed, Spain, Great Britain and Ireland have joined this club, with recent votes affirming support for Palestinian statehood, even as they bankroll UNRWA.

This contradiction is not merely symbolic. The refugee issue is one of the thorniest in the Palestinian-Israeli conflict. Five million Palestinian Arabs who are currently registered as "refugees from Palestine" (the two million in the West Bank and Gaza, plus two million in Jordan and another one million in Syria and Lebanon) demand for "return" to what they claim is their historic homeland. Were these five million Palestinians to join the nearly two million Palestinian Arabs who are already citizens of Israel, there would be a massive demographic shift. The Jews of Israel would be relegated to a minority. This is why the Israelis have consistently rejected the Palestinian "right of return." Yet, the Palestinians insist that this is a core demand in any peace agreement.

Lest anyone argue that the Palestinians do not take their demand for literal "return" seriously, it is worth reading a recent groundbreaking report by the International Crisis Group titled "Bringing Back the Palestinian Refugee Question." The report underscores the extent to which Western diplomats underestimate the importance that the Palestinians attach to this demand.

It also underscores the "almost supernatural significance" Palestinians attribute to UNRWA as embodying international support for their demand for a "return to Palestine."

Now that Sweden has assessed that Palestine meets the criteria of a state, is it prepared to address this longstanding Palestinian refugee narrative, along with UNRWA's role in perpetuating it? The way to do so would be to issue a clear statement that Palestinians living in Palestine (the West Bank and Gaza) would no longer be recognized as "refugees."

If the Swedes fail to take this simple and logical move, the implication would be that their recognition of Palestine is intended not to promote peaceful co-existence between Israel and Palestine, but rather to perpetuate dangerous and irredentist policies that have long characterized the Palestinian narrative, not to mention the refugee agency that purports to speak in its name.

Co-written with Jonathan Schanzer
Jerusalem Post
November 18, 2014

EINAT WILF

UN SECURITY COUNCIL PROPOSALS DAMAGE THE CHANCES FOR PEACE

Australia showed moral leadership in its term on the UN Security Council, most notably when it stood with the US in December and voted against a highly biased and anti-Israel draft resolution put forward by the Arab League, recognising true peace between Israel and the Palestinians can only be achieved via direct negotiations.

The path to Palestinian statehood has always passed through reconciliation with Israel – a recognition of both the fact of a Jewish state in the Middle East and the acceptance of its legitimacy.

The Palestinians don't need another UN Security Council resolution to achieve statehood in the West Bank and Gaza Strip. They could have it today by making peace with Israel. In fact, they could have had it in 2008 by accepting then-Prime Minister Olmert's peace offer, or in 2000 by accepting the American-brokered Clinton Parameters.

As such, one should be very sceptical of internationally imposed settlements. But, if the international community are determined an outside arrangement must be forced on the two sides, then their resolution must go all the way. Picking and choosing only some of the issues on which to stake a position is the worst possible course of action.

International proposals that include balanced-sounding banalities mixed with entirely unbalanced specific demands are guaranteed to fail.

The Security Council proposal was very specific on demands from the Israeli side, while leaving the obligations of the Palestinians and the Arab states up to a "fair and agreed solution." This left all the issues crucial to Israel up for negotiation, while whatever concessions Israel could have offered were already predetermined.

On the question of territory, the draft resolution called for a complete Israeli withdrawal to the pre-1967 lines with agreed, mutual swaps, seemingly rewarding the Palestinian choice in 2000 to reject the Clinton Parameters, while making no constructive counter-proposal and instead embarking on a suicide bombing campaign. On Jerusalem, it insisted on a "shared capital" for both states.

Such specific and unequivocal demands of Israel could have been paired with equally forceful statements renouncing the Palestinian demand for the "return" of the descendants of refugees from the 1948 war – which would effectively turn democratic Israel into an Arab country with a Jewish minority. But here, the resolution only asked for an "agreed, just, fair, and realistic" solution.

The resolution said it "reaffirms" the right of the Palestinian people to self-determination, but said nothing of the right of the Jewish people to self-determination in its historic homeland. It called for both states to be "independent, sovereign, and prosperous," and specified only for Palestine, but not Israel, that it must be "sovereign, contiguous, and viable." Israel, surrounded by an imploding Arab World and states who do not accept its legitimacy, has apparently no grounds for safeguarding its "viability."

The resolution "looks forward to welcoming Palestine as a full Member State of the United Nations," but did not look forward to the termination of all travel bans, cultural boycotts, and trade embargos on Israel maintained by the Arab States. It certainly doesn't condemn them as unacceptable, as it does with Israeli settlement activity. Furthermore, it makes no mention of Palestinian rocket attacks on Israeli civilians, nor mention suicide bombings.

Most reckless of all is the resolution's heedless indifference to Israel's security concerns. Where it is specific about Israeli concessions on territory, it was very vague about the "security arrangements" that will come after an Israeli withdrawal. The details, apparently, are to be worked out in future negotiations, but one detail is already built in: "a full phased withdrawal of Israeli security forces." Israel's concerns that the West Bank, which overlooks every major Israeli city and town, could become a base for Gaza-style rocket attacks were not even considered.

Moreover, issues that do require an international push got the most cavalier treatment in the text. Regional normalisation was broached as a general desideratum, but no specific demands were made and no deadlines or enforcement mechanisms were suggested. No guarantees were made of an international security force.

A bilateral process that would force both sides to come to terms with each other's respective, legitimate, occasionally overlapping, but sometimes fundamentally incompatible claims is the best path to a durable peace. To the extent that internationally imposed plans could succeed at all, it is by addressing all relevant issues in detail and in full. International proposals that include balanced-sounding banalities mixed with entirely unbalanced specific demands are guaranteed to fail.

Australia was wise to recognise this reality. Its national interests are best served by backing proposals that move the situation towards its declared policy goal of a two-state peace, not by seeking popularity in backing proposals that do the opposite.

Co-written with Shany Mor
The Sydney Morning Herald
February 15, 2015

EINAT WILF

WELL-MEANING COUNTRIES MAKE PEACE LESS LIKELY

When well-meaning people send destructive messages, even if unintentionally, it is worse than when those of ill will do. When Palestinian Authority President Mahmoud Abbas formally requests the U.N. General Assembly to pass tomorrow a resolution recognizing a Palestinian state in the West Bank and Gaza, with its capital in east Jerusalem, he will be counting on the support of more than one hundred member states. Most of those will be continuing their well-established tradition of voting against Israel, towards which their ill will is known, well documented and expected.

But some countries will be voting Yay, or sympathetically abstaining, in the hope that recognizing a state of Palestine would keep the two-state solution alive as the path to peace. Yet doing half the job is worse than doing nothing at all. In their vote, those countries of goodwill will be sending a dangerous message that would undermine, rather than increase, the chances for peace by privileging one aspect of the conflict while ignoring others.

For one, they will recognize east Jerusalem, home to the holiest sites to the Jewish people, as Arab Palestine, while glaringly omitting any parallel recognition of boringly residential west Jerusalem as Israel, even though both parts were deemed in the original partition resolution to be a "Corpus Separatum" that belongs neither to the Jewish nor the Arab state.

But the greater omission that would send a clear message that this vote in the United Nations is neither about peace nor a two-state solution is the issue of refugees. For 65 years, conferring refugee status on descendants of refugees from what became Israel following partition has been used as a tool of war. It has not only harmed the "refugees" themselves, who were encouraged to live their lives in the vain hope that one day they will be relocated to Israel, but was used to deny Israel legitimacy and peace. It was the means by which the Arab world expressed its rejection of the historic connection between the Jewish people and Israel, as well as the equal and legitimate right of the Jewish people to self-determination in the only land in which they were ever sovereign.

Well-meaning countries that truly care about peace cannot stoke the flames of conflict. They cannot seriously support a two-state solution at the same time that they condone, and even financially support, the perpetuation of hereditary refugee status for Palestinians.

Well-meaning countries that truly care about peace cannot stoke the flames of conflict. They cannot seriously support a two-state solution at the same time that they condone, and even financially support, the perpetuation of hereditary refugee status for Palestinians. To argue that five million Palestinians, who were never born in Israel, have the right to relocate there is incompatible with the survival of Israel, and an honest two-state solution. Especially after a Palestinian state is recognized, there is no logical or legal basis for maintaining the refugee status of Palestinians. A refugee, after all, is a person who cannot return to his country – not someone who is a citizen of one country but insists on being relocated to another. Nowhere in the world is refugee status conferred on a person who is a citizen of the country in which he resides. If well-meaning countries truly seek to turn the U.N. resolution into a tool of promoting peace, they need to address the conflict in its entirety. This means that Palestinians born and living in their own state, as well as those who have settled and have citizenship elsewhere, will no longer be accorded the status of refugees. It should be clear that not a dime be taken away from supporting those who have this status today and are in need, so that financial considerations are not used to excuse rejecting this proposal.

This would truly turn the resolution in the U.N. General Assembly into an instrument of hope and peace. It would send a clear message to the Palestinians that recognizing their state means also recognizing that the Jewish people have a full and equal right to theirs. After all, this was the original spirit of the General Assembly resolution of November 29, 1947, which Abbas wishes to revive. If the Arabs truly want to erase the mistake they made 65 years ago in rejecting that resolution, they should accept a proposal that seriously addresses the conflict in its entirety. If they finally do so, peace-loving Israelis and honest people everywhere would be able to believe again that peace is possible – and that would be an immensely powerful message of hope.

CNN
November 28, 2012

NOTE TO THE UNITED STATES: WE'RE NOT CHILDREN

The April 29 deadline set by U.S. Secretary of State John Kerry for securing peace and a Palestinian state has passed. And so, after all the back and forth of threats and demands, and the Fatah-Hamas unity deal announced last week, what have we been left with? A couple stuck in a toxic – but for a number of years not an extremely bloody and violent – relationship; a surprisingly enthusiastic counselor who has insisted, against the protests of the couple, on dragging them into counseling; signs of the violence to come as tensions start to rise again between the couple; and a breakdown of the counseling accompanied by a rebuke by the counselor, who laments that he can't want to fix the relationship more than the couple itself.

This is the story of the most recent round of failed Israeli-Palestinian negotiations. But while this latest push is interesting to dissect and discuss, it is secondary to the real issue, and the effort spent in the inevitable blame game following the breakdown of talks will prove pointless and futile. The fact is that the sides are miles apart. That is simply the way things are – and the two sides in this tug of war realize that better than anyone else.

The dispute between the Arabs and the Jews, between the Palestinians and the Israelis, and the story of the return of the Jewish people to their homeland, is unique and unparalleled in human history. The fact that the two sides are finding it difficult to reach a compromise and make the necessary "tough decisions," to quote the U.S. president, should therefore come as no surprise.

Israelis and Palestinians are not children – they are political players quite capable of making their own calculations and choosing alternatives that are the least bad from their own perspective.

Kerry, who took it upon himself to try to revive the talks, had initially set ambitious goals for the discussions, expecting no less than a full and final peace agreement between the sides by late this month. But while this quintessentially American spirit of "trying and failing is better than not trying at all" has helped make America great, in the Middle East – especially when it comes to the Palestinian-Israeli conflict – trying and failing is often far worse than not trying at all.

After all, trying and failing has historically sparked greater violence and deeper despair – just look at the intifada that followed President Clinton's failed peace efforts. In contrast, the years of stalemate that have characterized the Israeli and Palestinian situation prior to the forced renewal of talks under the stewardship of Kerry were some of the least violent and least bloody in decades of conflict, especially considering the mayhem the Middle East has been convulsed by in the wake of the so-called Arab Spring.

Granted, simply not killing each other is not the stuff that Nobel Peace Prizes are made of. But it is far better than being killed while negotiations are taking place. And, since the sides have been forced into negotiations, violence has escalated – just last week, Gaza-based militants fired half a dozen rockets into Israel on the last day of Passover.

Now, with Kerry's deadline having come and gone, the two sides have been rebuked by a visibly exhausted secretary of state. President Obama, meanwhile, noted that the sides have not demonstrated the political will to make "tough decisions." Yet, although these words might be true, as they say in the recently celebrated Passover Seder, *Ma Nishtana?* What has changed?

True, the two sides were not happy with the stalemate. Quite the contrary. But for both sides, it was better than the realistic alternatives – and certainly better than the bloody violence that both sides have been trying to avoid, violence that could be triggered again by risky compromises that have the potential to tear both societies apart.

At the end of the day, Israelis and Palestinians are not children – they are political players quite capable of making their own calculations and choosing alternatives that are the least bad from their own perspective. They might not always be the alternatives that outside observers think they should choose, but both sides should, as other peoples around the world are, be free to judge what is in their own interests. Both Israelis and Palestinians are also very much aware of the decisions they need to make if they are to come to a full and complete peace agreement, one that recognizes the right of both peoples to the land. If they don't make those decisions, it's not because they don't know what they are.

One day, when the geopolitical and political stars are aligned, peace will be possible. But until that moment comes, no amount of external prodding is going to make the two sides take decisions that they just aren't ready to make.

CNN
May 1, 2014

WINNING THE WAR OF WORDS

WHICH PALESTINE IS THE UN IN SOLIDARITY WITH?

Tomorrow, the United Nations marks the 'International Day of Solidarity with the Palestinian People.' But which version of the Palestinian state is the UN solidarity with? For there are two, and a choice must be made between them.

PALESTINE PASTS

Only twice in history was the territory between the Jordan River and the Mediterranean officially called 'Palestine,' and neither was for an Arab or Muslim entity of any kind. The first related to the end of Jewish sovereignty over the land, and the second related to its prospective renewal.

The Roman Emperor Hadrian was the first to make official use of the name 'Palestine' or 'Palestina' to refer to the region between the Jordan River and the Mediterranean. To secure the end of Jewish resistance to the Roman Empire he not only quashed their revolt and forced them into exile, but he dismantled the Province of Judea, as it was called at the time, and renamed it Palestina. This name was taken from the writings of the Greek historian Herodotus, referring to the Biblical and Egyptian 'Pleshet' or land of the 'Philistines' on the southern coast (near present day Gaza). During the following centuries of Arab and Ottoman domination of the region it was no longer called Palestine but the southern part of 'Al-Sham,' or greater Syria (the territory claimed now by the Islamic State).

The first version of Palestine is the state that could emerge in the West Bank and Gaza Strip. The second Palestine is the one which most Palestinian activists speak about, and, if realised, would mean the end of Israel as the sovereign state of the Jewish people.

The only other political entity in the Middle East to bear the name Palestine was the British Mandate, constituted in 1920 by the League of Nations, for the express purpose of effecting 'the establishment in Palestine of a national home for the Jewish people.' The mandate allowed Britain the option of cutting the territory east of the River Jordan out of the mandate for a Jewish national home, which it duly exercised two years later, with the creation of Transjordan, today's Jordan. This step actually further serves to emphasise the connection between the name Palestine and the project of Jewish national liberation in the historic homeland of the Jewish people: land which was now closed to Jewish settlement no longer bore the name Palestine, and Palestine itself had – from that point in 1922 until the end of the mandate in 1948 – the borders that today encompass Israel, the West Bank, and the Gaza Stip. These borders are often referred to 'historic Palestine.' Usually without mentioning that they are 'historic' only insofar as they lasted for barely three decades, were governed by a European superpower, and delimited as the future national home for the Jewish people.

In the years of the mandate, both Jews and Arabs in Palestine were referred to as Palestinians. There was a mass-circulation Arab daily called *Falastin* and a popular Jewish one called *The Palestine Post*. Jewish organisations as diverse as the Philharmonic and the fledgling Football League had the word Palestine in their names too.

WHICH FUTURE FOR PALESTINE?

Neither a restoration of Roman Palestine nor of British Palestine, however, is the intention of the International Day of Solidarity. Instead, its intended focus lies in the ambiguity between two other versions of Palestine, both potential states and both expressions of the self-determination of the Arab Palestinian people.

The first version of Palestine is the state that could emerge in the West Bank and Gaza Strip, those parts of Mandatory Palestine conquered by Arab armies in 1948 and subsequently by Israel in 1967. Nearly the entire international community supports the establishment of such a state, ideally as the outcome of peace negotiations with Israel. The establishment of a Palestinian Authority in 1994 following the Oslo Accords laid down the political infrastructure of such a future state: it already has a government, a flag, and its own stamps and passports; before its leadership rejected a final status agreement and embarked on a suicidal (in every sense of the term) terror campaign in 2000.

The second Palestine is the one which most Palestinian activists speak about, and, if realised, would mean the end of Israel as the sovereign state of the Jewish people. It would be an Arab state on the entire territory between the Jordan

River and the Mediterranean Sea, and come into being by superseding and erasing the present State of Israel. The borders of such a Palestine can be seen in the logos of all the leading Palestinian organisations – 'radical' and 'moderate' alike. This is the Palestine of the demonstrators who chant, 'From the River to the Sea, Palestine will be free.' It is the Palestine that activists imagine when they demand 'Justice for Palestine,' a code phrase for bringing an end to Israel as the sovereign state of the Jewish people – the injustice that those Palestinians seek still to correct. It is the Palestine to which the Arab refugees from the 1947-1949 war and their millions of descendants today demand to 'return' so that the Jewish people would no longer have a sovereign nation in which they are a majority. The fate of any Jewish minority left in such a Palestine would be even worse than that of Jewish minorities in other Arab countries in the past century, if only because the persecuted Jews of Iraq and Yemen and North Africa had the State of Israel to flee to.

These two versions of Palestine differ not just in their territorial ambitions, but in their essence. The first is a project of national liberation which would confer upon a currently stateless people the self-determination it should have attained more than half a century ago by the necessary acceptance of a parallel project of national liberation next door. The second is a project of national elimination, directed against the same neighbouring project, under the genuine belief that the most important goal is not the attainment of a state for the Palestinian people but the denial of one for the Jewish people.

WINNING THE WAR OF WORDS

Which Palestine does the International Day of Solidarity promote? The text of the original 1977 resolution, drafted in the era of automatic Soviet and Arab-backed majorities in the UN General Assembly and with references to the 'inalienable rights of the Palestinian people including the right of return' leaves little doubt as to the original intention. And the rhetoric of today's activists is, if anything, even more menacing.

At the same time, the date chosen for the International Day of Solidarity, whatever the original intentions might have been, opens an option for a more constructive kind of solidarity. On 29 November 1947, the UN General Assembly voted to end the British Mandate over Palestine and replace it with two sovereign nation-states, one Arab and one Jewish – neither had a name yet. The Jews accepted this plan and endeavoured to build their state, which declared independence on the last day of the mandate nearly six months later. The Arabs rejected partition and embarked on a war of extermination against the Jewish population of Palestine – and lost.

Perhaps, on this Day of Solidarity we can acknowledge the fact that this choice, not just the rejection of the specific partition plan of 29 November 1947, but the obsessive and violent rejection of Israel in any form, has been a terrible mistake. The world faces a choice: solidarity with liberation Palestine or with elimination Palestine. It must choose the former.

Co-written with Shany Mor
Fathom
Autumn 2014

PALESTINIAN MOVES TO JOIN ICC HAVE NOTHING TO DO WITH JUSTICE

Recent Palestinian moves to join the International Criminal Court are one more step in the decades-long campaign to vilify Israel and brand it in world opinion as "evil incarnate". It is a direct continuation of the "placard strategy" of anti-Israel activism, whereby Israel and Zionism are equated – whether in demonstration placards, speeches or writings – with a series of words: colonialism, apartheid, ethnic cleansing and genocide. These words are not chosen because they somehow reflect reality but because they are universally considered evil.

The effect of the continuous repeating of Zionism/ Israel = Evil is to create an intellectual environment in which physically ridding the world of Israel would be considered desirable, even noble.

The purpose of the Palestinian moves in the ICC is to achieve official international sanction for branding Israel with the term "war criminal", thereby adding an internationally sanctioned legitimacy to the placards used to vilify Israel and Zionism.

The purpose is not to seek justice by bringing certain Israeli officials to trial before the ICC but achieving an officially sanctioned international consensus that Israel, as a whole, is a war criminal country. As such, the resulting implication is that its entire existence is illegitimate.

WINNING THE WAR OF WORDS

Israel is concerned about Palestinian accession to the ICC because it knows that no matter what it has done, what it does and what it will do, it will be found guilty.

This is a process that renowned human rights activist and former Canadian justice minister Irwin Cotler has named "laundering": the campaign to delegitimise Israel and Zionism is "laundered" through the international human rights institutions. Given that this is the deep purpose of the Palestinian efforts to join the ICC and prosecute Israel through it, any effective response must address this deeper issue, rather than the issue on the surface: the ostensible legal battle.

Israel has invested substantial diplomatic capital in trying to prevent the Palestinians first from joining the ICC and now in trying to prevent the ICC from accepting their status as a full-fledged state.

The most common interpretation of the Israeli efforts to prevent the Palestinians acceding to the ICC is that Israel is afraid of being "found out". Most people assume that if Israel had nothing to hide it would not be so concerned; ergo, it has something to hide from the ICC. The ICC tries war crimes, meaning therefore that Israel must indeed be a "war criminal country" if it is so concerned about it. The Palestinians are achieving the goals of their ICC campaign – to vilify Israel in international opinion – before they have even been accepted to the ICC.

But Israel's concerns about Palestinian accession to the ICC are not about being "found out" but rather about the failure of the UN and international treaty system of human rights to give Israel a fair trial. This is one of the greatest failures of the UN and treaty-based system of human rights. There is no justice for Israel in the UN. There is definitely no justice for Israel in the Orwellian-named Human Rights Council. And there will be no justice for Israel in the ICC.

Israel is concerned about Palestinian accession to the ICC because it knows that no matter what it has done, what it does and what it will do, it will be found guilty.

The UN system and the international judicial system are structurally incapable of fairly judging Israel because they are numbers-based systems: one country, no matter how vile, one vote.

Israel has one vote. The Arab League countries have 21, the Muslim countries have 56. They have voted, and will always vote, against Israel. With such a high share of the votes they get still more countries to support them.

The outcome of this simple maths is that in all the UN bodies where the US cannot exercise its veto power, Israel remains alone, unprotected, and is regularly ganged up on by the countries that have the preponderant numbers.

Half of all condemnations issued by the UN Human Rights Council have been against Israel, equal to the rest of the world combined. Moreover, the condemnations against Israel are always absolute, whereas condemnation against other countries is usually softened with caveats and commendations for their supposed efforts to do better.

The same is true of the UN General Assembly – half of its decisions historically have been directed against Israel. The ICC, which has failed to establish itself as an impartial and credible body, is likely to do no better if it were allowed to attempt to judge and punish Israel.

The tragic irony is that much of the UN and its treaty-based system of human rights was created to counter the darkness of the Holocaust, then grossly misinterpreted and abused against the world's only Jewish state, Israel.

The Australian
February 11, 2015

Chapter 3

A VISION FOR PEACE

"The Jewish people around the world and Palestinian people around the world are both indigenous to the Land of Israel/Palestine and therefore have an equal and legitimate right to settle and live anywhere in the Land of Israel/Palestine, but given the desire of both peoples to a sovereign state that would reflect their unique culture and history, we believe in sharing the land between a Jewish state, Israel, and an Arab state, Palestine, that would allow them each to enjoy dignity and sovereignty in their own national home. Neither Israel nor Palestine should be exclusively for the Jewish and Palestinian people respectively and both should accommodate minorities of the other people."

Al Monitor
March 6, 2014

"The historical connection between the Jewish people and their land points to a possible transformation of Israel and the story of Israel in the context of the 'Arab Spring.' In this new context, the perception of Israel in the Middle East might change from that of a colonial foreign insert to the national expression of the Jewish people, indigenous to the region."

Turkish Policy Quarterly
Spring 2014

"Herzl's own conception of Judaism was so secular and national that he felt religious Muslims, Christians, and Jews could all be Zionists. He thought the Jewish state should be akin to the French state, allowing people to have different religious faiths or none at all. So, at least as conceived by Herzl, Zionism was not meant for the Jews alone, and non-Jews could partake in it."

The Tower Magazine
September 2014

AN ISRAELI LEFTIST FINDS A GLIMMER OF HOPE

I was born into the Israeli left. I grew up in the left. I was always a member of the left. I believed that the day that the Palestinians would have their own sovereign state would be the day when Israel would finally live in peace. But like many Israelis of the left, I lost this certainty I once had.

Why? Over the last 14 years, I have witnessed the inability of the Palestinians to utter the word "yes" when presented with repeated opportunities to attain sovereignty and statehood; I have lived through the bloody massacres by means of suicide bombings in cities within pre-1967 Israel following the Oslo Accords and then again after the failed Camp David negotiations in 2000; and I have experienced firsthand the increasing venom of anti-Israel rhetoric that only very thinly masks a deep and visceral hatred for the state and its people that cannot be explained by mere criticism for the policies of some of its elected governments.

But one of the most pronounced moments over the past several years that has made me very skeptical toward the left were a series of meetings I had with young, moderate Palestinian leaders to which I was invited by virtue of being a member of Israel's Labor Party.

I realized that, contrary to the leftist views in Israel, which support the establishment of a Palestinian state because the Palestinians have a right (repeat: right) to sovereignty in their homeland, there is no such parallel Palestinian "left" that recognizes the right (repeat: right) of the Jewish people to sovereignty in its ancient homeland.

I had much in common with these young Palestinian leaders. We could relate to each other. However, through discussion, I soon discovered that the moderation of the young Palestinian leaders was in their acknowledgement that Israel is already a reality and therefore is not likely to disappear. I even heard phrases such as, "You were born here and you are already here, so we will not send you away." (Thank you very much, I thought.) But, what shocked and changed my approach to peace was that when we discussed the deep sources of the conflict between us, I was told, "Judaism is not a nationality, it's only a religion and religions don't have the right to self-determination." The historic connection between the Jewish people and the Land of Israel was also described as made-up or nonexistent.

Reflecting on the comments of these "moderates," I was forced to realize that the conflict is far deeper and more serious than I allowed myself to believe. It was not just about settlements and "occupation," as Palestinian spokespeople have led the Israeli left to believe. I realized that the Palestinians, who were willing to accept the need for peace with Israel, did so because Israel was strong. I realized that, contrary to the leftist views in Israel, which support the establishment of a Palestinian state because the Palestinians have a right (repeat: right) to sovereignty in their homeland, there is no such parallel Palestinian "left" that recognizes the right (repeat: right) of the Jewish people to sovereignty in its ancient homeland.

These did not remain personal reflections. For the following years, these conversations impacted my political career as I found myself within the Labor Party increasingly alienated from what I began to term as the "self-flagellating left," to which the conflict was entirely due to Israel's actions and which demanded no responsibility or recognition from the Palestinians. As a member of the Knesset, on behalf of the Labor Party, I helped carry out a split within the party between its dovish and hawkish wings in order to allow the hawkish wing headed by then-Defense Minister Ehud Barak to remain in the coalition with Prime Minister Benjamin Netanyahu. This realization has also motivated my continued work around the world to defend Israel and Zionism, insisting that all peace must be rooted in the mutual recognition of the equal right of both peoples to the land.

So, it was somewhat ironic when, just several months ago, I received an email from the Israeli-Palestinian meeting's organizer to write a response to one of the program's core funders as to whether the program had an "impact on anything or anybody." I was asked to "reflect back a few years" and to write whether the program "had any impact on you – personally, professionally, socially, politically..." Naturally, I responded. I wrote that the program had a "tremendous impact on my thinking and I continue to discuss it to this day in my talks and lectures." I shared the above story with the organizer, recognizing that "it is probably not a perspective you want to share with your funders."

In response, the organizer sent me an email saying that there are "many, not one, grass-roots and political Palestinians who truly believe that Jews have a right to part of the land." I responded enthusiastically that meeting even "one Palestinian who believes that the Jewish people have an equal and legitimate claim to the land would be huge for me," and that "I've been looking for someone like that ever since I participated in the program many years ago."

Shortly thereafter, I received the following quote from a Palestinian participant who expressed a desire to renew the program so that "we can reach a resolution to this conflict by having an independent Palestinian state with East Jerusalem as its capital living in peace side-by-side with the State of Israel." I responded, "I do not see that this individual writes that he recognizes the equal and legitimate right of the Jewish people to a sovereign state in their own homeland." I was then asked to write precisely what would convince me that we have a true partner for peace in the Palestinians. So, I drafted the following phrase:

"The Jewish people and Palestinian people are both indigenous to the Land of Israel/Palestine and therefore have an equal and legitimate claim to a sovereign state for their people on the land." I added that this sentence could be expanded to say, "Both the Jewish people and the Palestinian people around the world have an equal and legitimate claim to settle and live anywhere in the Land of Israel/Palestine, but given the desire of both peoples to a sovereign state that would reflect their unique culture and history, we believe in partitioning the land into a Jewish state, Israel, and an Arab state, Palestine, that would allow them each to enjoy dignity and sovereignty in their own national home." I would also add here that it should be clear that neither Israel nor Palestine should be exclusively for the Jewish and Palestinian people respectively and both should accommodate minorities of the other people.

The organizer promised to get back to me. Weeks and months passed, and I was about to publish this piece, opening up the conversation, hoping to find partners who share my belief, so that I could rekindle my hope that peace is possible. At the last minute, I was contacted by professor Mohammed S. Dajani Daoudi, the head of American Studies at Al-Quds University and founder of the Palestinian centrist movement, Wasatia. All he asked was to change the word "claim" to "right," and "partition" to "sharing," saying that "right" was more positive, and "partitioning" had in the deep psyche of the Palestinians the negative connotation of the 1947 UN partition plan recommendation. He emphasized that 67 years later, he hopes that Palestinians would realize that sharing the land by a Jewish state and a Palestinian state, as envisioned by the UN resolution, was "the right thing to do" in 1947, since both people do have a legitimate right to the land, and remains "the right thing to do" today. I found these changes wholly acceptable and welcome. So the statement we share now reads as follows:

"The Jewish people around the world and Palestinian people around the world are both indigenous to the Land of Israel/Palestine and therefore have an equal and legitimate right to settle and live anywhere in the Land of Israel/Palestine, but given the desire of both peoples to a sovereign state that would reflect their unique culture and history, we believe in sharing the land between a Jewish state, Israel, and an Arab state, Palestine, that would allow them each to enjoy dignity and sovereignty in their own national home. Neither Israel nor Palestine should be exclusively for the Jewish and Palestinian people respectively and both should accommodate minorities of the other people."

Who else will join us in our journey to find true partners on both sides?

Al Monitor
March 6, 2014

CAN PALESTINIANS ACCEPT THE EXISTENCE OF A JEWISH STATE – FOR PEACE?

As Israeli and Palestinian negotiators begin a new round of talks, one question will hover in the air: Is there an agreement to be made? Some will express hope. Most will express skepticism. But to answer this question, one must delve deeper into the far greater question of the root cause. We need to know what we are fighting over. What are we killing and being killed for? To attempt to resolve the conflict, we must first know its essence.

The key question is whether at its core, the conflict is rational or existential. A rational conflict is about resources and their fair division.

If our conflict is rational, then it emerges from the simple fact that two peoples live on one land, and therefore need to find a way to share it. A rational conflict should be amenable to rationally negotiated solutions, based on the principle of partition – dividing the land between two states, one for each of the two peoples, one Jewish, one Arab – as has been the governing theme of all negotiation efforts since 1937. Sooner or later, such a solution should bring peace and an end to the conflict.

But increasingly, Israelis, myself among them, have come to wonder whether the essence of the conflict is quite different – not rational, but existential. Is the conflict about the very existence, rather than the size, of the State of Israel?

The Palestinian Arabs have refused any solution that would create a state for themselves, if the price of doing so meant finally accepting that the Jews should have their state, too.

On Feb. 18, 1947, British Foreign Secretary Ernest Bevin, not an ardent Zionist by any stretch of the imagination, addressed the British parliament to explain why the UK was taking "the question of Palestine," which was in its care, to the United Nations. He opened by saying that "His Majesty's government has been faced with an irreconcilable conflict of principles." He then goes on to describe the essence of that conflict: "For the Jews, the essential point of principle is the creation of a sovereign Jewish state. For the Arabs, the essential point of principle is to resist to the last the establishment of Jewish sovereignty in any part of Palestine."

Bevin's description of the "irreconcilable conflict" is telling. He does not argue that the Jews and Arabs in Palestine can't agree about how to rationally and fairly divide the land. He explains that the Jews want a state – of whatever size – and that the Arabs want the Jews not to have a state at all. This is an existential conflict by definition, as it involves the very existence, rather than the size, of the state of the Jewish people. Such a conflict is indeed irreconcilable, barring the annihilation of the State of Israel, and as Bevin concluded, "There is no prospect of resolving this conflict by any settlement negotiated between the parties."

Bevin's description of the conflict is more than 66 years old, but the majority of Israelis today wonder if the situation has truly changed. The reason that I myself have become more skeptical of the rational conflict thesis is that in the past decade, it has become even more evident that Bevin's prescient description has been the best predictor of Israeli and Palestinian decisions since 1947. Whereas the Jews wanted a state, whatever its size, they have repeatedly and at all critical junctures accepted and continue to accept solutions that embrace, even if begrudgingly, the logic of partition. And, whereas the Arabs have opposed the Jews having any state at all, at all critical junctures and up to this moment, they have refused any solution that would create a state for themselves, if the price of doing so meant finally accepting that the Jews should have their state, too.

If people are to be judged by their actions – as I believe they should – then over time, the existential thesis better explains why the Palestinian Arabs would prefer to have nothing rather than the dignity of their own state, if it means sharing the land with the state of the Jewish people. Most of the Western world continues to believe that the essence of the conflict is rational, and therefore doggedly pursues rational negotiated solutions based on the principle of partition. But if the essence of the conflict is existential, peace would only be achieved the day the Arabs accept the deep logic of partition, which is that the Jewish people have an equal and legitimate right to a sovereign state in the only land in which they were ever sovereign. The rest is details.

Al Monitor
August 15, 2013

ISRAELIS WANT GENUINE PEACE, NOT A PEACE PROCESS

I am writing the following as a citizen – not as an analyst of Israeli and regional politics, and not as a politician with a worldview. I am writing the following as an Israeli citizen who sits in cafes with friends, buys pizza for her children and gets stuck in traffic behind buses: The renewal of talks between Israelis and Palestinians fills me with dread.

Analysts of the peace process, pleased by their renewed relevance, speak of the guarded hope, general skepticism and mostly indifference of Israelis and Palestinians, who believe little will come of the renewed talks. What I feel is neither hope, nor skepticism, nor indifference.

For more than 20 years, peace talks meant more terrorism and more death. The more serious the talks got, the greater the number of violent deaths.

The closer the negotiations came to addressing the core issues that have been tearing apart Israelis and Palestinians for decades, the worse the violence became. The more gut-wrenching the decisions that were discussed, the more the crazies on both sides emerged from their holes to kill, maim and send all chances for peace up in flames.

For more than 20 years, peace talks meant more terrorism and more death. The more serious the talks got, the greater the number of violent deaths.

Negotiations for peace have become so associated with terrorism that in the 1990s, its victims were called "victims of peace." We on the left, myself included, were so obsessed with peace that we insisted that negotiations continue despite the vicious acts of terrorism, as proper tribute to those "victims of peace."

But peace should have no victims, and neither should the road to achieving it.

I listen in dread to the men who tell me how important it is that negotiations resume. I listen to the analysts, politicians and retired security chiefs argue in baritone voices, their confidence unmarred by years of being wrong, that the stalemate in the peace talks was dangerous, that the status quo could not endure and that a third bloody intifada was about to break out if negotiations did not resume.

The fact that the data did not support their supposedly obvious claims did not seem to bring about any sense of responsibility, humility or measure of self-doubt. The fact remained that the longer the stalemate continued, the less we were killing each other. During the last few years without negotiations, the number of Israelis and Palestinians killed as a result of violent conflict between them has been the lowest in decades, perhaps even in the entire history of the conflict.

True, a stalemate is not heroic. It is not accompanied by handshakes on manicured lawns. No one gets a Nobel Peace Prize for merely preventing Israelis and Palestinians from killing each other. But for Israelis, as well as Palestinians, the stalemate of the past few years has meant life.

So I question whether negotiations are good in and of themselves and whether we should aspire to their resumption no matter what. I wonder if it is right to cheer those who push the two sides to the negotiating table when they are not certain that they will emerge from the negotiations with an agreement that ends the conflict and the killing. The aphorism that trying and failing is better than not trying at all does not apply, because trying, and certainly trying and failing, means going back to a time when there was fear in going to cafes and buying pizzas and terror in getting stuck in traffic behind a bus.

I know that the right thing to do is to applaud the renewed negotiations, but before we go down this path, I wanted to share the feelings of one citizen who dreads their renewal and feels that this time around, if she has to choose between peace and life, she will choose life.

Al Monitor
August 1, 2013

TOWARDS A ZIONISM OF INCLUSION

Theodor Herzl's original vision for Zionism included Jews, Christians, and Muslims living in harmony with a shared purpose. The history of Zionism tells us that this moment may not be too far off.

One would be hard-pressed to find an allegation that has not been leveled at the Jewish people's movement for self-determination in their homeland: Zionism is racism. Zionism is colonialism. Zionism is apartheid. No social evil has been missing from the placards raised at anti-Israel and anti-Zionist demonstrations, all claiming "Zionism = X."

These allegations have been exposed time and again as libels and smears, but even the greatest defenders of Zionism have failed to notice a much more positive, and indeed remarkable, facet of this century-old ideology: Zionism = Inclusion.

That is to say, Zionism was, is, and will likely continue to be on a steady trajectory of increasing inclusiveness. Contrary to those who say Zionism is an exclusivist ideology, from the moment of its foundation it was one of the world's most inclusive national and political movements.

This is not to argue that the Zionist inclusiveness has been one of singing "Kumbaya" with open arms. Zionism became inclusive because it was necessary for its survival. Its inclusiveness was, originally, largely due to pragmatic considerations. Only later did it become inherent in the ideology itself. Without inclusiveness, Zionism would have died in infancy.

In its early years, Zionism was a marginal and radical movement among the Jewish people. In 19th century Europe, Jews mostly responded to the hostility of their host countries by attempting to assimilate into European society or immigrating to the United States. Few considered the restoration of Jewish sovereignty in the Land of Israel as a serious alternative. Many even viewed it as a threat to their efforts at assimilation. So from its very beginnings, Zionism could not afford to exclude anyone. If it were to survive, anyone willing to rally to its flag would be welcome.

The realization that inclusiveness was critical to Zionism's survival dawned on its founder, the writer and dramatist Theodor Herzl, as he sought support for his ideas among the Jews of Europe. Herzl's initial vision for a renewed Jewish state was a kind of Vienna in the Levant, a Central European utopia on the banks of the River Jordan. The intended audience for his vision was Jews such as himself – cultured, assimilated, and European – who would create a better Europe in the Middle East. A Europe that, unlike the real one, would be a place where Jews could feel safe, hold any position in society, and never need to question their sense of belonging.

It was to these Jews that Herzl turned when he wrote his manifesto, *The Jewish State*. He appealed to them in Britain, France, Germany, and the Austro-Hungarian Empire. But after repeated attempts, he was dismayed to find they were not interested. Worse still, they rejected his ideas by asserting that they were solely British, French, German, or Austro-Hungarian. As the writer Amos Elon noted, the response to Herzl in Vienna was, "We Jews have waited two thousand years for the Jewish state and it had to happen to me?"

Like most Jews of Central and Western Europe, who saw themselves as modern and enlightened, Herzl despised the Jews of the East. In his eyes, they were primitives stuck in medieval times, resistant to the Enlightenment and decidedly un-European. He certainly did not think they could carry the mantle of Zionism and build the state he envisioned. The last thing he wanted for a Jewish state was to replicate the *shtetl* life of Eastern Europe and Tsarist Russia. But even as Herzl was being rebuffed by the cultured Jews of the West, he was, as Elon wrote, "surprised by the resonance of his tract in the East; he had expected it to strike hardest in the assimilated West, not in the East, which he regarded as backward, even primitive." But the Eastern European Jews were the ones who embraced Zionism. They were inspired by his vision. They wanted to be the builders of the new state. And they were willing to do what it took to resurrect Jewish sovereignty in the blistering heat of the Land of Israel.

Touring Europe with his vision, whether among the *shtetl* immigrants of London or the Jews of Bulgaria, Herzl was overwhelmed by the reception.

> News of his passage had preceded him. When the train stopped at the station an enormous crowd of Bulgarian Jews hailed the author of The Jewish State as their long-awaited savior.... People rushed to kiss his hand, and in the synagogue he was placed by the

altar. He did not know how to face the crown without turning his back to the holy Torah. But a man called out: "It is all right for you to turn your back to the altar. You are holier than the Torah...." With his magnificent beard, his glowing eyes, his proud frame, and fine, simple gestures, Herzl stood on the stage, looking "as kings wish to look but seldom do."

He was received by the Jews of the East like the Messiah who would take them back to the land of their ancestors.

Overwhelmed by this reception, Herzl the writer realized that the time had come for rewriting. He recast the Jews of Eastern Europe as the true national Jews. He wrote them into his story as those who had kept their sense of being a nation while the assimilated Jews of the West had not. In Herzl's rewritten narrative, the Jews of Eastern Europe became better suited to the task of building a Jewish state than anyone else; because they, above all others, knew what it meant to be a nation; and Zionism was first and foremost about the national revival of the Jewish people.

During the first Zionist Congress, Elon writes,

> The Russian Jews had left the deepest impact [on Herzl]. Warm hearted, soulful, eminently practical, deeply steeped in folk tradition, which in the East was still very much alive, they had none of the identity problems of the Western Jews, none of his sense of alienation. Herzl had previously thought of them as poor, oppressed candidates for relief, living in a

"primitive" East; it took the congress to open his eyes: "How ashamed we felt, we who had thought that we were superior to them. Even more impressive was that they possess an inner integrity that most European Jews have lost. They feel like national Jews but without narrow and intolerant conceit.... I had often been told in the beginning, 'The only Jews you'll win will be the Russian Jews.' Today I say, 'They would be enough!'"

Indeed, over the next three decades, the Jews of Eastern Europe became the primary adherents of the Zionist vision and the ones who built its foundations against overwhelming odds. By embracing them and rewriting his narrative to reflect their enthusiasm for the cause, Herzl demonstrated that, for Zionism to survive, it would need to include everyone who supported it. He also showed how to achieve this: By rewriting the story to include the previously excluded group; and to do so in a way that not only included the new group, but made it one and the same with the Zionist vision.

Inclusiveness has many forms, and different countries and ideologies have found different ways of accomplishing it. France has a secular republican model under which anyone can become French if they adopt the values of the republic, live in a secular public sphere, keep competing identities such as religion to the private sphere, and embrace French culture and language. America has a post-national model that depends heavily on embracing the principles of the constitution and the "American way of life." Britain has a post-colonial model under which peoples and religions are united under the scepter of the queen. All models of inclusion in countries that claim to be inclusive are problematic. All of them are partial. All suffer from a gap between the claim to inclusion and the reality. And all are challenged by groups who do not accept the "rules for inclusion." In that sense, Zionist inclusiveness is no different. But its mechanism is.

The Zionist mechanism is one of retelling and rewriting its story as if Zionism was always designed to include a previously excluded group. This mechanism is not one of simple assimilation, "multiculturalism," or even the "melting pot." It is a constant rewriting of the story of Zionism so that a new story emerges to erase the old, thus creating the sense that Zionism has always been able to include the previously excluded group.

This is no different from the way all human beings adapt to changing circumstances. We write and rewrite our histories. We take moments of failure, despair, and rejection, and remake them into stories of growth, transformation, and triumph. We create a unified narrative that makes sense out of everything that has happened to us. We tell ourselves it had to happen so we could become who we are today. Internally, almost all humans – except for the clinically depressed – are like Pangloss, the perennially optimistic philosopher in Voltaire's *Candide*.

The Zionist mechanism works in the same manner. It is a constantly retold story, but at any given moment it is also a unified one. It is not a legalistic mechanism of "neutral" citizenship in a "neutral" state, where abiding by the law is the only requirement and all who abide by the law are equally included. The Zionist state believes in equality before the law, but Zionist inclusiveness works in a very different way: *Zionist inclusiveness is about the story, not the law.*

Zionism adapts by rewriting the story to include the previously excluded group, doing so in a way that not only includes the new group, but makes it one and the same with the Zionist vision.

One of the most remarkable examples of Zionism's ability to rewrite its story and transform its narrative is its relationship to the Holocaust. This narrative transformation has been achieved so completely that almost everyone now believes the State of Israel was born as a direct result of the Holocaust, and owes its existence to the tragedy and its survivors. To understand the magnitude of this transformation, we need to appreciate how difficult it was for Zionism to deal with the Holocaust.

Zionism was first and foremost an ideology of activism. It was a rebellion against Jewish passivity in exile, a rejection of the Jews' resigned attitude toward their fate as a persecuted and marginalized minority. As a secular movement, it rebelled against simply waiting for the Messiah. It called for the Jewish people to be their own Messiah, to go by themselves to the Holy Land to restore Jewish sovereignty, rather than waiting for God's anointed to do it for them.

In addition, Zionism contained an element that called for the total negation of Jewish life in exile. This, however, was not true for all Zionist thinkers. Herzl, for example, imagined that the re-establishment of Jewish sovereignty would also contribute to the life of Jews in exile by relieving them from the status of a stateless people at the mercy of the nations. He described in his novel *Altneuland* ("Old-New Land") that with the establishment of the Jewish state, "Jews who wished to assimilate with other peoples now felt free to do so openly, without cowardice or deception. There were also some who wished to adopt the majority religion, and these could now do so without being suspected of snobbery or careerism, for it was no longer to one's advantage to abandon Judaism."

Herzl thought that Jews would be able to walk proudly as equals among the nations once they had a state, even if they did not become its citizens. But as the situation in the Diaspora became more severe and ultimately genocidal, the choice made by many Jews to remain in Europe was scorned. For many Zionists, the growing strength of their embryonic state and the growing danger faced by the Jews of Europe delegitimized life in the Diaspora.

The negation of the exile (*shlilat ha'galut* in Hebrew), as it became known, was not just about negating the legitimacy of Jewish life in the Diaspora, but also negating its very essence. Zionism created an entire series of opposites expressing this: Active vs. passive, strong vs. weak, proud vs. humiliated, self-sufficient vs. dependent, healthy vs. sick. Zionism came to be seen as a cure for the sickness inflicted upon Judaism by the exile.

So when the Holocaust occurred, it was an affront to Zionism's core ideology. The Jews who perished in the Holocaust represented everything that Zionism wanted to change. The victims were seen as passive, going to their deaths like "lambs to the slaughter." They were weak, dependent, and suffered the greatest possible humiliation – an industrial genocide. Whenever they rebelled, it was because they were Zionists. The Warsaw Ghetto resistance fighters, for example, became national heroes, in part because they were members of Zionist youth movements preparing to immigrate to Israel. The survivors were even worse in the Zionist perception. They were suspect simply because they had survived. The suspicion was that they must have engaged in deceitful and treacherous actions in order to do so.

Herzl's own conception of Judaism was so secular and national that he felt religious Muslims, Christians, and Jews could all be Zionists.

The nascent State of Israel took the Holocaust survivors in and recruited them to fight for its independence. This was, again, a pragmatic inclusiveness. Israel needed them to survive. But it did not want to hear their story, and it found no place for them in the Zionist narrative. At best, they served as Exhibit A of why there could be no Jewish life in exile. They were the negative to Zionism's positive.

Beginning with the public trial of Adolf Eichmann in 1961, however, the people of Israel not only started to listen to the survivors, but to rewrite the story of Israel and Zionism accordingly. It did not happen quickly, but over the next few decades, the story of the Holocaust and its survivors became so integrated into the story of Zionism that many today believe the Holocaust is the reason for Israel's existence. This has become such a dominant story that many people around the world – including Jews and Israelis – are barely aware of the history of Zionism and the pre-state Zionist community that preceded the Holocaust.

The survivors of the Holocaust eventually became Israel's new heroes. Not just the Zionist resistance fighters, but any and all who survived. Just this past Holocaust Remembrance Day, Twitter and Facebook were taken over by photos of soldiers with Holocaust survivors, who were hailed as Israel's true heroes.

The retelling of Zionist history to incorporate the Holocaust and its survivors is now complete. Zionism genuinely stripped itself of its scornful attitude toward the survivors, and achieved complete inclusiveness by transforming its narrative.

Another major group is still in the process of undergoing narrative inclusion: The Jews who immigrated to Israel from Arab countries. Prior to the Holocaust, they were a tiny minority of the Jewish world. Only one million out of a world total of 18 million Jews resided in North Africa and the Arab Middle East. With colonialism ending and the impending establishment of the State of Israel, tensions between the Muslim Arab population and the Jews rose. Over the course of only a few years, these Jewish communities – which in most cases predated Islam – were removed. A large number of the Jews fleeing these countries found refuge in the newly created State of Israel.

Much like survivors of the Holocaust, the Jews from Arab countries were recruited into the Zionist state-building effort, but they were not welcomed or included in any real sense. They were viewed as being "not us" – "*nicht unsere*" to use the Yiddish term. For decades, they suffered overt and covert discrimination. But they slowly found themselves, mostly through their own struggle and effort, becoming part of Israeli society, to the point that they all but became Israeli society. To a great degree, this inclusion was achieved through marriage. When I speak to large groups of Israeli students or soldiers I like to conduct a little exercise. I ask how many among them have four grandparents of the same ethnic origin. Usually, in a room of 200, less than ten hands will be raised.

Many will no doubt claim that, with all due respect to the achievements of Zionism, it has never sought or succeeded in including non-Jews. It is one thing to include all the Jews in the world – an impressive feat in itself – but quite another to include non-Jews.

First, it is important to note that Herzl's own conception of Judaism was so secular and national that he felt religious Muslims, Christians, and Jews could all be Zionists. He thought the Jewish state should be akin to the French state, allowing people to have different religious faiths or none at all. So, at least as conceived by Herzl, Zionism was not meant for the Jews alone, and non-Jews could partake in it. Throughout *Altneuland*, Herzl emphasized, "The fundamental principles of humanitarianism are generally accepted among us. As far as religion goes, you will find Christian, Mohammedan, Buddhist, and Brahmin houses of worship near our own synagogues." In his vision of a future Jewish state, "Religion had been excluded from public affairs once and for all. The New Society did not care whether a man sought the eternal verities in a temple, a church, or a mosque, in an art museum, or at a philharmonic concert." Herzl's ideal as stated in *Altneuland* is "We do not ask to what race or religion a man belongs. If he is a man, that is enough for us." In the novel, in fact, it is exclusionary Jews who are portrayed as the main enemy.

Many Soviet immigrants to Israel are an example of Herzl's idea in action. Though they could claim citizenship due to their Jewish ancestry, many were not Jews themselves, and some were practicing Christians. Yet their immigration to Israel was considered highly valuable – even one that "saved" the country. In fact, when their status as non-Jews did became an issue – such as the burial of fallen soldiers – it was met with anger from the broader Israeli society, indicating that, for most Israelis, they belonged fully and unquestionably.

Over recent decades, Israel has also sought to include its Druze and Bedouin communities. The initial reason was, again, pragmatic; in this case, the need for soldiers. As early as Israel's War of Independence, many Bedouin and the entire Druze community joined the Jews in fighting off the invading Arab armies. From that moment, the Druze and many Bedouin were included in the Israel Defense Forces. Since then, Druze and Bedouin military heroes have been hailed by Israeli society and media. Indeed, during the latest conflict with Hamas, a Druze senior commander became a media hero after he demanded to be sent back into the field despite severe injuries. Many Druze self-identify as not merely Israelis, but also Zionists. This is not to say that there are no problems with discrimination or other issues, but it does show that Zionism is willing to embrace those who align themselves with it, whether Jewish or non-Jewish. Indeed, it seems that Zionism only finds it difficult to include non-Jews when they embrace competing Arab or Palestinian national identities. Zionism in itself can include non-Jews in its story, so long as they do not align themselves with a hostile narrative.

The current frontier of inclusion is that of ultra-Orthodox Jews and Israeli Christians. In the past, Israeli Christians by and large adopted Arab and Palestinian identities. Christians were among the most important thinkers and shapers of modern Arab and Palestinian nationalism, and often its most zealous adherents. This is due, in part, to their status as a minority among Arab Muslims. In recent years, however, as the Arab Spring revolutions have placed the lives of Middle Eastern Christians in jeopardy, Israeli Christians have begun to explore the possibility of an Israeli rather than Arab Christian identity. As Arab identity is increasingly perceived as exclusively Muslim and even openly hostile to Christians, Israeli identity has emerged as a new possibility for identification. Like the Druze and Bedouin, this is being explored through service in the IDF, as more and more voices in the Christian community look to military service as a means of engaging with "their state." In response, the IDF is taking steps to make military service more accessible. This process has only just begun and is politically controversial, but it demonstrates again that Zionism is willing and capable of integrating non-Jews who do not embrace a competing identity hostile to Zionism.

The next frontier of Zionist inclusion is adapting the story to fit Christians, ultra-Orthodox Jews, and ultimately Muslims.

Ultra-Orthodox Jews, for their part, have had an ambivalent relationship with Zionism from the beginning. Zionism was a thoroughly modern movement that believed human beings should shape their own fate, rather than passively accept the will of God. In addition, it was composed of mostly secular and even atheist Jews who rebelled against the religious way of life. As a result, many ultra-Orthodox thinkers saw Zionism as heresy. Some extreme ultra-Orthodox sects even claimed that Zionism was an affront to God and an obstacle to the realization of God's plans for the Jewish people, so only by destroying the State of Israel can the arc of history be put right again.

Yet the Holocaust left the surviving ultra-Orthodox Jews in need of refuge, and many found it in the State of Israel. Nonetheless, even ultra-Orthodox Israelis have found it difficult to come to terms with the existence of a secular Jewish state, and especially with its success. Moreover, unlike Zionists who believed that sovereignty was essential to Jewish survival and prosperity, the ultra-Orthodox felt that their exile posed no threat to the future of the Jewish people, and might even be preferable.

For most of Israel's existence, the Zionist majority was willing to let the ultra-Orthodox maintain their way of life and remain on the margins of Israeli society. But in recent years, as the ultra-Orthodox community has become much larger, more and more Israelis feel that the status quo cannot be sustained. In particular, they believe ultra-Orthodox Jews' heavy dependence on the welfare state, low participation in the labor force, and almost non-existent military service places an unfair burden on other Israelis.

So began the battle to include ultra-Orthodoxy in the Zionist narrative. Initially, it took the form of a demand for military service and greater participation in the labor force. In other words, the motivation was once again pragmatic. Zionism wants the ultra-Orthodox to be taxpayers and soldiers. But over time, it is likely that the mechanism of narrative transformation will begin to operate. The Zionist story will be rewritten so as to make ultra-Orthodoxy into another, equally genuine form of Zionism. The 2,000-year-long continuing existence of ultra-Orthodox communities in the holy cities of Jerusalem, Hebron, Safed, and Tiberias, for example, may be portrayed as having paved the way for modern Zionism and secured the path for the return of the Jewish people to their homeland.

The last frontier of inclusion is unquestionably that of Israel's Muslims, who currently describe themselves as Arab Palestinian Muslims holding Israeli citizenship, and it is the most difficult. At the moment, it seems almost ludicrous to think about their future inclusion in the Zionist narrative. Israeli Muslims themselves are likely to see the idea as an affront to them and their sense of Arab-Palestinian national identity. But I would like to present the possibility that, sometime in the future, such inclusion could take place.

Currently, the Palestinian national movement and Zionism appear so at odds that it is nearly impossible to conceive of a situation in which the Zionist narrative could be sufficiently rewritten to include Israeli Muslims. The furthest that most Israeli Muslims are willing to go in this direction is to demand a "neutral" Israeli state, stripped of any signs or symbols of being Jewish or Zionist. The argument put forth by them and especially their leadership is that as long as the state of Israel continues to be Jewish or Zionist, Muslims can have legal rights, but will never truly be a part of Israeli society.

As a result, for many Israeli Muslims, the only path to full inclusion and belonging is an end to Zionism. In the current situation, this is somewhat understandable. If Zionism and Palestinian nationalism are in direct conflict, the embrace of one naturally implies the rejection of the other. But it is also, of course, impossible for Zionism to accept, since it demands not the rewriting of the Zionist story, but the burning of the book itself.

As a result, the inclusion of Israeli Muslims in the Zionist narrative is likely to happen under one of two extreme conditions: Full peace between Israel and the Arab world, or an Arab world so engulfed in chaos and brutality that Israeli Muslims distance themselves from an Arab Palestinian national identity in search of an alternative. Under one of these extreme but not impossible scenarios, Israeli Muslims would no longer be Arab Palestinian nationalists, but Israelis and Zionists.

Should either of these scenarios materialize, the obstacles to inclusion would be lifted, at least in principle. One could begin to imagine the Zionist narrative being retold so that Israeli Muslims are fully included in the story. This inclusive narrative could be about how Muslims tended and kept the land for centuries, welcoming the returning Jews to share it for the good of all. It could be the story of how local traditions of generous hospitality led the local Muslims to provide refuge to the Jews coming to their shores. It could be a story with new heroes – Jews and Muslims who exemplified cooperation long before it was the norm; Muslims who protected Jews from harm; Muslims who sold land to the Jews and shared valuable agricultural knowledge with them; and

Muslim teachers who taught about Zionism without neglecting their own side of the story.

It could be a narrative that resurrects the buried history of Muslim support for Zionism in Palestine. This history was recently uncovered in Hillel Cohen's book *Army of Shadows: Palestinian Collaboration with Zionism*, which covers the many dissident elements in the Palestine Arab Muslim community that viewed Zionism positively – as Herzl had hoped – and even assisted it through land sales, intelligence, and military assistance against the British. It could be a story that reminds us of heroes like Haifa mayor Hassan Bey Shukri, who wrote to the British government in 1921,

> We strongly protest against the attitude of the said delegation concerning the Zionist question. We do not consider the Jewish p changed for light and transient causes; and accordingly all experience eople as an enemy whose wish is to crush us. On the contrary, we consider the Jews as a brotherly people sharing our joys and troubles and helping us in the construction of our common country.

It could perhaps become the story of how the Muslims, together with Jews, made the Land of Israel whole again, bringing together all the religions that originated and flourished within its borders. It could be a story of return and reunification. A story of how the Muslims had to come to terms with being a minority and the Jews with being a majority before both could truly live as one, introducing the key element in any drama of return and reunification: The overcoming of obstacles.

It must be left to far better storytellers than myself to imagine what this narrative might look like. Right now, it requires the most fanciful imagination. But if Zionism has taught us anything, it is that reality begins with a dream.

The Tower Magazine
September 2014

Chapter 4

TELLING OUR STORY

"Before it could be staged before a live audience, the story of a resurrected Jewish state had to be told and retold; and it is only through this storytelling that Israel became a reality. Those who founded Israel, built it, fought and sacrificed for it, did so because they were inspired by a grand idea and a magnificent story."

The Tower Magazine
April 2014

"Truly effective and long-lasting *hasbara* is about explaining the ideas and circumstances that formed the foundation of Israel's existence. And there is a growing audience for this. It only seems that we live in an ADHD world of sound bites, of crude black and white 'analysis', of simplistic notions of good and evil. Actually, I find that people want so much more than that. They want to understand, to appreciate complexity, to really 'get it'."

Fathom
Spring 2014

WINNING THE WAR OF WORDS

THE SEARCH FOR A SINGLE ZIONIST STORY

My generation grew up with an Israel divided against itself. Now two great writers have tried to heal with words, and the results are deeply moving.

The modern state of Israel was born in the mind of an ecstatic playwright named Theodor Herzl. It was an idea, a story, and a drama long before it became the physical reality that it is today. Before it could be staged before a live audience, the story of a resurrected Jewish state had to be told and retold; and it is only through this storytelling that Israel became a reality. Those who founded Israel, built it, fought and sacrificed for it, did so because they were inspired by a grand idea and a magnificent story. They were the writers of their own epic drama.

From the beginning, the success of Zionism and Israel depended on the ability to tell a great story. The drama of the return of the biblical people to the biblical land moved Christians in Britain and across Europe to support the nascent Zionist movement. The story of constructing a perfect society from scratch sustained young pioneers in the difficult land of Israel, and attracted socialists and utopian thinkers of all kinds. The icon of the phoenix, of a nearly extinguished people reborn into a new life of self-rule, inspired nations and peoples to rally to the cause of the newly established Jewish state.

These stories sustained Israel and Zionism over a century of struggle unparalleled in the history of any nation. But my generation has grown up wondering whether these stories are still relevant, still powerful, and still capable of motivating people to action. We came of age at a time when the foundational stories of Israel and Zionism were torn apart, revised, overturned, and attacked as illegitimate. Given the gift of individual freedom and choice, but bereft of a unifying story that gives meaning to those choices, we have been left to fend for ourselves. My generation celebrates an Israel that is diverse, fascinating, colorful, and messy; an Israel that acknowledges the many different views and perspectives of those who inhabit it. We do not want to return to a time when many were excluded in the name of unity. But we also mourn the loss of a grand, inspiring narrative.

For Israel and Zionism to survive and thrive over the next one hundred years, a new story must be written and told; a single story that has room for all its characters and inspires all who hear it. Acclaimed Israeli writers Yossi Klein Halevi and Ari Shavit have attempted to do just that in their new books, *Like Dreamers* and *My Promised Land*, and though each approaches the task from a dramatically different angle, both of them succeed.

These are two very different books by two very different men. Interweaving the stories of a group of paratroopers who helped reunited Jerusalem in 1967, Halevi's *Like Dreamers* traces the history of Israel and the divergent ideologies that shaped it from the Six-Day War to the present. Shavit's *My Promised Land* takes a wider view, telling the story of the "triumph and tragedy" of modern Israel from early Zionism to the present day through a wide range of individual stories. For both authors, Israel's journey through the 20th century and into the 21st is also their own. Fourth-generation Israeli Ari Shavit and first-generation immigrant Yossi Klein Halevi are both deeply and profoundly Israeli, and so are their books. They struggle with what being Israeli means for them personally and how they fit in into Israeli society. Born only four years apart (Klein Halevi in 1953, Shavit in 1957), both men have embarked on writing their life's work in order to resolve the question of their own personal identities. By telling the story of Israel through the lives of others, they are also struggling to decipher the meaning of Israel to their own lives.

Both authors begin with the mysterious entanglement of Jewish fear and Jewish power in modern Israel. Klein Halevi tells of his sense of dark foreboding as a young American following the events leading up to the Six-Day War. "My father and I shared the same unspoken thought: again. Barely two decades after the Holocaust, the Jews were facing destruction again. Once again, we were alone," he writes. And then, as if to echo the sudden reversal of fate, immediately tells how "Israel reversed threat into unimagined victory." His elation is still palpable all these years later as he describes how Israel "not merely survived, but reversed annihilation into a kind of redemption, awakened from our worst nightmare into our most extravagant dream."

In the opening of *My Promised Land*, Shavit echoes Klein Halevi's feeling of anxiety. He confesses that "for as long as I can remember, I remember fear. Existential fear." But then, after detailing numerous instances of existential fear from 1967 on, he also confesses, "For as long as I can remember, I remember occupation," recounting the manner in which Israel's great victory turned "my nation" into an "occupying nation."

Klein Halevi and Shavit are haunted by these reversals and extremes. They struggle to reconcile success and failure; triumph and tragedy; the pride and the shame that are Israel and Zionism. They both understand that the decade of reversals from 1967 to 1973 to 1977, and especially the trauma of 1973, "threw the Israeli psyche out of balance." They both try to restore this balance through the personal. It is as if they have given up on any possibility of intellectually explaining Israel, Zionism, and the great revolutions of modern Jewish history. To them, Zionism and Israel are life, and just as human life is better told than explained, they try tell the story of Israel in the only way possible: Through its people.

Klein Halevi focuses on the stories of seven IDF paratroopers whose lives are so representative of Israel's changes and struggles that they seem too good to be true. His protagonists are the kibbutzniks Arik Achmon, Udi Adiv, Meir Ariel, and Avital Geva; as well as the religious-Zionists Yoel Bin-Nun, Yisrael Harel, and Hanan Porat. These were the paratroopers who breached the gates of the Old City to become the first citizens of a sovereign Jewish state in two thousand years to stand on the Temple Mount and touch the stones of the Wailing Wall. They are the same paratroopers who, in an act of near-insanity, dared to cross the Suez Canal during the 1973 Yom Kippur War and turned it into Israel's Stalingrad, turning the tide toward an Israeli victory.

Even though Klein Halevi himself admits that his protagonists belong to a very small and socially homogenous group – Ashkenazi men born in the 1940s – through the seven of them and their families and friends, he is able to chronicle the entire political, ideological, economic, and cultural spectrum of Israel: from Left-wing anti-Zionism to Right-wing messianic imperialism, high-flying capitalism to spartan socialism, militant atheism to religious dogmatism, Tel Aviv hedonism to yeshiva asceticism, *avant-garde* conceptual art to mystical Jewish poetry. He tells the tale of their ideological battles and their fraternity in war, of that which drove them apart and later brought them back together.

Klein Halevi's protagonists, like their country, are not stagnant; they transform over time. They act upon their country and are acted upon by it. Yoel Bin-Nun, a Haifa-born yeshiva boy and a "stubborn disciple" of the charismatic Rabbi Zvi Yehuda Kook, helped found the settlement movement, and later broke with it in "grief and rage" following the assassination of Prime Minister Yitzhak Rabin, his torment aiding in the country's healing.

Udi Adiv, a member of Kibbutz Gan Shmuel, denounced "Israel's plan for an imperialist war" against Egyptian leader Gamal Abdel Nasser in 1967, broke with the far-Left Matzpen movement due to its support for a two-state solution, traveled to Damascus after the Munich Olympic massacre of 1972 to help the PLO create an anti-Zionist terrorist underground composed of Jewish and Arab Israelis, served twelve years in prison for it, completed his Ph.D. in London, and finally found himself back in Israel as a humdrum anti-Zionist academic – no longer so unique.

From the beginning, the success of Zionism and Israel depended on the ability to tell a great story.

Yisrael Harel, born in 1939 in Central Europe, "the worst place and time for a Jew," came to Israel as a refugee living among native-born Sabras and a religious boy in socialist, militantly secular Haifa. He longed from early childhood to be part of the "elite of sacrifice" and realized this dream by helping found the Movement for the Complete Land of Israel, organizing religious-Zionists, and giving the movement a voice as editor and key writer of the settler journal *Nekudah*.

Meir Ariel, who drove a tractor in the cotton fields of Kibbutz Mishmarot and "distinguished himself in the paratroopers as a misfit," achieved instant fame in 1967 after writing the anti-war song "Jerusalem of Iron," but struggled for years to achieve recognition for his subsequent work and explored all modes of life and living. In *Like Dreamers*, he emerges as the Bob Dylan of his generation, giving voice to both anti-war cynicism and Jewish mysticism.

Hanan Porat established the first West Bank settlement in Kfar Etzion immediately after the Six-Day War and, after being wounded in the Yom Kippur War, went on to found the activist settler movement Gush Emunim – "Bloc of the Faithful" – with Yoel Ben-Nun and Yisrael Harel; but unwittingly found himself increasingly identified with the more extreme wing of the movement.

Avital Geva, the only one who remained a kibbutznik throughout, continued to insist on the relevance of socialism and, in the process of constantly searching for new ways to make it relevant to the younger generation, pushed his fellow kibbutzniks to think about their collective mission, and then (accidently) became a leading ecological conceptual artist.

Arik Achmon, who as a child tried his best to be "an exemplary kibbutznik," ended up leaving his kibbutz as a young adult when his brand of Mapai socialism was denounced by the Stalinist majority. He then devoted his life to the military and becoming a hero of the Jewish people. Eventually, he broke with the "utopian nostalgia" of the kibbutz, seeking to introduce modern capitalism to Israel so that it might become the "great nation it could be."

In telling the stories of these men, Klein Halevi achieves a remarkable feat. He writes a work of non-fiction that reads like a work of fiction. His storytelling is so skilled that the reader wonders whether Klein Halevi happens to be an extremely lucky storyteller, finding seven remarkable life stories that closely track the life of the nation, or whether he simply made it all up (he didn't).

EINAT WILF

If Halevi tells the story of Israel by leading a chamber orchestra, Ari Shavit conducts a Wagnerian opera in seventeen acts, each one given a short title and date. "At First Sight, 1897" follows the journey of Shavit's great grandfather to the Land of Israel. "Into the Valley, 1921" chronicles the passionate founding of the first major kibbutz. "Orange Grove, 1936" tells the story of Israel's 1930s prosperity and the moment of Zionism's "utopian bliss." "Masada, 1942" deals with the forging of Zionism's old-new myth of survival in the face of Arab attacks. The harrowing chapter on "Lydda, 1948" digs deep into a painful historical wound: The deportation of the city of Lydda's Arab population during the War of Independence. Shavit's rendering of the story is intense to the point that even the most indifferent reader will cry "enough!" "Housing Estate, 1957" tackles the creation of a new Israel out of huddled masses of poor refugees. "The Project, 1967" is about Israel's nuclear program. "Settlement, 1975" deals with the settler movement. "Gaza Beach, 1991" relates Shavit's own experience as a reserve soldier guarding jailed Palestinians. "Peace, 1993" tells the tragic history of Israel's peaceniks. "J'accuse, 1999" grapples with the discontents of Israel's Sephardi Jews. "Sex, Drugs, and the Israeli Condition, 2000" reports on Tel Aviv hedonism. "Up the Galilee, 2003" is concerned with Israel's Arab citizens. "Reality Shock, 2006" chronicles Israel's sense of impotence during the Second Lebanon War. "Occupy Rothschild, 2011" is about Israeli innovation and industry. "Existential Challenge, 2013" is about the nuclear threat from Iran. And finally, in "By the Sea," Shavit traces his great-grandfather's journey through Israel and reflects on an alternative possible history for him and his family. If Klein Halevi follows his protagonists wherever they go, even quite regular moments, Shavit calls his actors on stage to bellow grand and majestic arias. Some of the characters who appear are well-known, such as Shas party leader Aryeh Deri, who exemplifies "the oriental revolt" of the Sephardi Jews; or Yossi Beilin, who personifies the rise and fall of the Israeli peace camp. But more frequently, it is lesser-known characters, such as Shavit's great-grandfather and accidental Zionist Herbert Bentwich, or the forger of the modern Masada myth Shmaryahu Gutman, and even imagined characters like "the orange grower," who tend to steal the show.

Among the lesser-known subjects are female Sephardi journalist Gal Gabai, whose pain is evident as she speaks of not quite belonging, of how even though "we have no other home, Israel is not quite home," because Israel "was not really meant for us." Due to the extermination of European Jewry, she says, "we were imported here and we were imported late." And then there is the "ultimate Israeli" Kobi Richter, who never questioned whether or not he belonged, telling us, arrogantly but accurately, that "when Israel was about the kibbutz, I was on a kibbutz; and when Israel was about the military, I was in the military; and when Israel is about high-tech, I am in high-tech." Indeed, he actually says of his service as one of Israel's top fighter pilots, "It's not that I played Tom Cruise; Tom Cruise played me."

As the reader is introduced to more characters and more stories, each very different from the other, it becomes clear that Klein Halevi and Shavit have been driven to write by a very different kind of existential fear than the one with which they open their stories: The fear that internal schisms will lead to Israel's demise.

Klein Halevi speaks of his father, who believed that "the great weakness of the Jews was the temptation of schism, even in the face of catastrophe." Shavit writes of the seven "revolts" against early, spartan, activist Labor Zionism: The settler, peace, liberal-judicial, oriental, ultra-Orthodox, hedonist-individualistic, and Palestinian revolts. But while "each and every one of these upheavals was justified, the outcome of these seven revolts was the disintegration of the Israeli republic," and from a certain point on "they became petty and dangerous."

Their books are a desperate search for unity amidst the differences that are tearing Israeli society apart. They both deeply desire to achieve *e pluribus unum* – out of many, one. Klein Halevi's father tells him that when the Jews are united "no enemy could destroy us." Toward the end of his book, Shavit desperately asks, "Can 21st century Israel reconstruct the Mount Herzl republic?" and speaks of the "Herculean mission" to "unify a shredded society."

Both Klein Halevi and Shavit write of these schisms in general terms, but it is clear that they are also deeply personal. Both have lived through the fraying of Israeli society. Both have witnessed in their own personal lives the ways in which

Israeli society has been pulled and torn apart. They have lived through the age of unity of pre-1967 Israel, real or imagined, and watched in horror as it became fragmented and divided. They belong to the generation that witnessed firsthand Israel's various "revolts," and stood helpless when an Israeli prime minister was assassinated for his politics. Whereas my generation has grown up amidst these "revolts" with no memory of unity, except for the mythological one told though the nostalgic, rose-colored glasses of our parents, Klein Halevi and Shavit remember enough to seek to recreate it.

In their quest to forge unity from diversity and heal these schisms, Klein Halevi and Shavit wield the tools of their trade, the trade that has made Zionism and Israel possible – storytelling. But they tell their stories in very different ways. Klein Halevi's storyteller is a quiet healer; Shavit's is a fierce surgeon.

Klein Halevi writes his book in the soft light of dusk, when the setting sun bathes even the most dilapidated buildings in a warm glow. His sentences are soft and mellow, such as when he describes how the veterans of Kibbutz Ein Shemer trusted Avital Geva with the future of their community, "because he understood that without constant watering and pruning, this miracle conjured from the void would wither." One can sense the pride of the old kibbutzniks as "they saw in Avital and his friends their own vindication. In a single generation – from Poland to Ein Shemer – the kibbutz had created young people who seemed to lack even a genetic memory of exile."

Shavit's book, however, is written in the harsh Israeli sun, under which all are exposed. Shavit's phrases are full of sharp juxtapositions and contradictions. When describing the pioneers of Kibbutz Ein Harod, he describes their sense of urgency:

> As Jewish Europe has no more hope, Jewish youth is all there is. It is the Jewish people's last resort. Here it will be revealed whether the ambitious avant-garde is indeed leading its impoverished people to a promised land and a new horizon, or whether this encampment is just another hopeless bridgehead to yet another valley of death.

Even though Shavit is secular, his book reads like a Catholic confession – the story of a sinner who seeks salvation by speaking honestly and openly of his sins. Shavit is brutally honest throughout the book about the history of Zionism. He burrows mercilessly into its most painful wounds. He does so because after decades of struggle, he is seeking peace of mind and wants to restore balance to the Israeli psyche. Even though his book is about the stories of others, it is his personality that emerges throughout. In it, Shavit – whose public persona is one of seriousness, gravitas, and level-headedness – reveals himself as a tempestuous youth, fluctuating between euphoric highs and depressing lows. He is high on early Zionism, reveling in its triumphs, its utopianism, its youth, and its oozing sexiness. Even when Zionism turns brutal when faced with the Arab revolts of 1936-1939, one cannot mistake Shavit's admiration for the "merciless determination" of those who forged a "community of combat," realizing that it was about "us or them, life or death," and whose spirit was "never to retreat, never to rest, always to push forward."

But Shavit is also deeply anxious, even angry, about Israel and Zionism's current condition. "Israel had become a state in chaos and a state of chaos," he says. He is especially angry with the Israeli elite; the old ones who have "turned their back on the state they felt they had lost, and the new, rebelling forces never bothering to create a dedicated, meritocratic elite of their own." And yet, as he confesses his sins, he still wants recognition for Zionism's achievements and affirmation that not all is lost. He reminds us that "Zionism was about regenerating Jewish vitality," and that "people that have come from death and were surrounded by death, nevertheless put up a spectacular spectacle of life."

At the end of his confession, he still wants Israel and Israelis to be loved for who they are as they are. He tells the confessor that "we are not only creative and innovative, but authentic and direct and warm and genuine and sexy," adding that "our grace is the semi-barbaric grace of the wild ones."

My generation celebrates an Israel that is diverse, fascinating, colorful, and messy; an Israel that acknowledges the many different views and perspectives of those who inhabit it. We do not want to return to a time when many were excluded in the name of unity. But we also mourn the loss of a grand, inspiring narrative.

If Shavit provides the confession, it is Klein Halevi who forgives. Although religious himself, Klein Halevi writes like a compassionate agnostic, accepting the grand impossibility of knowing anything for certain in this life. Even though the paratroopers are all his elders, Klein Halevi himself emerges from the book as the all-forgiving father whose wayward children have returned. They have travelled, they have strayed, but he does not judge the follies of their youth. He looks upon them with love and simply tells their stories so that their children, as Klein Halevi writes in the dedication to his own children, will be able to write "the next chapter."

It is only through the prism of Klein Halevi's compassionate confessor that both Udi Adiv's decision to travel to Damascus to assist an anti-Zionist terrorist plot, and the messianic euphoria that accompanied the establishment of the settlement of Ofra right in the midst of Arab Samaria, can be understood in context. It is only when Klein Halevi tells how Hanan Porat – who as a four-year-old boy was forced out of his home and saw most of his childhood friends orphaned when his kibbutz, Kfar Etzion, was conquered by the Jordanian Arab legion and razed to the ground – returned after 1967 to rebuild the demolished community that it becomes impossible to think of Porat as an "illegal settler."

When Klein Halevi recounts the story of how Yoel Bin-Nun, who at the age of twelve confessed to a girl that his deepest longing was for "the Temple to be rebuilt"; was present at the age of 21 at the now-famous speech by Rabbi Zvi Yehuda Kook on the eve of the Six-Day War, in which the rabbi cried out against the Arab occupation of ancient Jewish sites such Jerusalem, Hebron, and Jericho; and then found himself one of the first Israelis to stand atop the Temple Mount a few short weeks later; even a committed atheist can understand why Bin-Nun saw the hand of God in the 1967 victory, and why he felt that "Jewish history had vindicated Jewish faith." It is through Klein Halevi's prism that one finds compassion for all Israelis struggling to make sense of the momentous events – sometimes lasting no more than a few days – that have marked their entire lives.

At the end of their stories, both tellers have told the story of Israel – and it is indeed one. Klein Halevi is the weaver at his machine, painstakingly creating a single cloth and pattern from the wildly divergent lives of his protagonists. Detail after detail, almost without noticing, a magnificent tapestry emerges on the other side. It is a picture that encompasses everyone, Left and Right, religious and secular, capitalist and socialist – a pattern in which Israel is "the partial fulfillment and partial failure of the contradictory dreams" of his protagonists.

Shavit, in contrast, creates one Israel by breaking it apart and laying bare its constituent parts for all to see. Beautiful and ugly, proud and shameful, black and white, no grays whatsoever, they shine in the glaring sun. And as the reader closes the book and takes a step back, a picture of one Israel emerges. One Israel where all parts belong, all parts make sense, and all parts are necessary. One Israel that "offers the intensity of life on the edge."

EINAT WILF

Klein Halevi and Shavit are those rare beings who are lovers of Israel and defenders of Zionism, yet are not blind to the faults of the object of their affection. Through their stories they have given young Israelis the greatest gift: A story in which they can find themselves and of which they can be proud. And with that gift, a future can be built.

The Tower Magazine
April 2014

ZIONISM DENIAL

As Israel marks its national Holocaust Remembrance Day, many around the world will secretly roll their eyes. "There they go again the Zionists, using their precious Holocaust to justify their state, their power, their faults, reveling in a world guilted into silence."

There are those who believe, too many, that without the holocaust there would have been no Israel. Most of them make this assumption in good faith. The American President himself, in his June 4, 2009 Cairo speech, spoke of "the recognition that the aspiration for a Jewish homeland is rooted in a tragic history that cannot be denied."

But when so many believe that without the Holocaust there would have been no Israel, those who want Israel erased from map and memory, or isolated as an illegitimate state come to resent the Holocaust, or at least its association with Israel.

The American President wanted to make an important stand against Holocaust denial in the capital of the Arab world. He did not understand that by reaffirming the dangerous equation that the global legitimacy for Israel is rooted in the Holocaust, he fanned the motivation to engage in Holocaust denial for those who continue to believe, as they always have, that Israel is not a legitimate state.

Holocaust denial, Holocaust minimization ("6 million is an exaggerated number") Holocaust "equalization" ("there were other genocides and ethnic cleansings, the Holocaust was no different"), Holocaust reversal ("what the Nazis did to the Jews is what the Jews are doing to others"), Holocaust marginalization ("other people were also killed in the War") and Holocaust by association ("the Palestinians are the secondary victims of the Holocaust"), are all but different facets of the same effort – to rob Israel of what seems like a powerful and indisputable source of legitimacy.

To portray Israel as the outcome of the Holocaust is to engage in Zionism Denial. It robs the Jews of their agency, their history, their historical connection to the Land of Israel and their yearning to return to it.

The deceptively seductive canard that "the Palestinians are the secondary victims of Europe's crimes" is one of the worst of all these lies, since to the untrained ear it sounds logical. In this tale, after World War II, when it became clear that the Final Solution was not final and the Jewish survivors could not be expected or welcomed to stay in Europe the Europeans decided to "dump" the surviving Jews on unsuspecting Arabs who were living in an area that colonial Europe controlled.

This convenient solution for Europe resulted in the displacement of hundreds of thousands of Palestinians who have been homeless and occupied ever since. Ergo, the Palestinians are the secondary and still uncompensated victims of Europe's crimes against the Jews.

Israel exists not because the Europeans dumped the surviving Jews in the colonially controlled Middle East. Israel exists because the Jews willed it into existence. The modern state of Israel exists because the Jews who created it believed themselves to be descendants of the Israelites and Judeans who were sovereign there in ancient times and paid a high price for preserving their separate existence as a people. The modern state of Israel exists because for centuries and millennia Jews kept yearning for Israel, ending the Passover Seder with the words, "next year in Jerusalem."

The modern state of Israel exists thanks to visionary Jewish thinkers and leaders who realized that changing times created an opportunity to turn the messianic hope to return to Israel into a political program, and who were able to mobilize sympathy and support in critical junctions for their project. President Obama finally got it right when in his speech to AIPAC on March 4, 2012 he spoke of Shimon Peres as having had "his heart always in Israel, the historic homeland of the Jewish people."

In fact, if it were not for Arab resistance and Britain's betrayal and submission to Arab pressures, the Holocaust as such might not have taken place. Jews would have been able to escape Europe to their ancient homeland in what was already a widely supported embryonic state. They would have had a destination country to which to immigrate freely at a time when Hitler was still willing to let the Jewish people go.

Israel came into being after World War II not "thanks" to the Holocaust, but thanks to Britain's imperial dissolution. Just as India and Pakistan required no Holocaust to attain their independence and come into being, so too Israel.

To think that only the act of absolute evil against the Jews could legitimate a state for the Jews is to deny the Jews what is taken for granted for all others. The Jewish people would have achieved their state sooner or later as part of the wave of liberation of peoples around the world. Their vision, determination, industry and willingness to fight for their state would have ensured it.

To portray Israel as the outcome of the Holocaust is to engage in Zionism Denial. It robs the Jews of their agency, their history, their historical connection to the Land of Israel and their yearning to return to it. It erases all that was dreamt, written, done and achieved by the Zionists before World War II. It turns Israel into a colonial project of guilty Europeans rather than a national liberation project of an indigenous people reclaiming their homeland. In remembering the Holocaust, Israel mourns not only all that was and still is lost, but Zionism's greatest tragedy and failure.

Israelis do not "revel" in the Holocaust as a source of legitimacy for their state. They mourn a vision of a state that could have been home to so many more. Zionism sought a state for the Jews not so that "never again." Zionism sought a state for the Jews so that never at all.

The Daily Beast
April 17, 2012

PRESIDENT OBAMA'S LESSON IN ZIONISM

Thanks to President Barack Obama, Zionism is back. Much was made in the international media of Obama's appeal to the Israelis to pursue peace, especially in his address to the students. But perhaps the greater significance of the president's visit is that the entire trip, as well as his appeal to peace, constituted an intensive course in Zionism 101.

At a time when the Turkish prime minister calls Zionism "a crime against humanity" and The New York Times provides a platform for undermining it, the liberal Obama reminded the world of Zionism's foundations and nature as a movement of liberation and self-determination.

He did so in words. He did so in gestures.

Within moments of landing in Israel, Obama emphasized that the creation of the state of Israel is rooted in the historical, yet sometimes denied, link between the Jewish people and the Land of Israel: "I know that in stepping foot on this land," he said, "I walk with you on the historic homeland of the Jewish people. More than 3,000 years ago, the Jewish people lived here, tended the land here, prayed to God here." Later, Obama gave form to his words by visiting the Dead Sea Scrolls, to witness firsthand the ancient biblical texts written in Hebrew, uncovered in Israel.

Obama then made the leap into modern times, recognizing that Israel is the fulfillment of the Jewish people's dream to be "masters of their own fate in their own sovereign state." Obama visited the grave of Theodore Herzl, the founder of modern Zionism, saying that Herzl "had the foresight to see that the future of the Jewish people had to be reconnected to their past." Obama honored and paid tribute to the political program of the Zionist movement to establish a homeland for the Jewish people in the Land of Israel: "The dream of true freedom finally found its full expression in the Zionist idea – to be a free people in your homeland. That's why I believe that Israel is rooted not just in history and tradition, but also in a simple and profound idea – the idea that people deserve to be free in a land of their own."

Obama reminded the world that Zionism is an inspirational idea and a movement that, if properly understood, could help bring peace between Israel and the Palestinians and shape for the better a changing Arab world.

Obama also reversed his well-intentioned but misguided message in his 2009 Cairo speech that "the aspiration for a Jewish homeland is rooted in a tragic history" of Jewish persecution, which culminated in the Holocaust and led to the state of Israel. "Here, on your ancient land," Obama said while visiting Yad Vashem, "let it be said for all the world to hear: The state of Israel does not exist because of the Holocaust."

These days, between Holocaust Memorial Day and Israeli Independence Day, Obama's words keep resonating. His emphasis on the Jewish people actively taking their fate into their own hands to create the state of Israel demonstrated a deep understanding of Zionism's true nature. He reminded the world that Zionism is an inspirational idea and a movement that, if properly understood, could help bring peace between Israel and the Palestinians and shape for the better a changing Arab world.

As long as the world in general, and the Arab world in particular, believes that the state of Israel is a form of "compensation" to a suffering people by a guilty world, a false lesson is learned that victimhood is rewarded. This encourages a problematic race to the bottom to be perceived as the world's most oppressed, a strategy that some Palestinians have been perfecting for decades, manifested in the choice to remain refugees within their own borders and defining their existence by "indignities" committed by Israel, rather than engaging in actions that will lead to their own dignity.

If the Palestinians and the Arabs were to properly understand Israel and Zionism through Obama's recent encapsulation of it, they might finally begin to engage in a race to the top toward self-determination and the assumption of responsibility to shape their own fate. Palestinians can have a state tomorrow if they behave like the Zionist leaders – saying a pragmatic yes to what they can get, even if it is far less than they feel is justly deserved.

Obama explained in his visit to Israel that the reason the United States and Israel stand together is a "common story: patriots determined to be a free people in our land, pioneers who forged a nation, heroes who sacrificed to preserve our freedom, and immigrants from every corner of the world who renew constantly our diverse societies." The Palestinians too can stand together in this common story if they look toward the future instead of the past, and begin in the task of their own nation building, rather than another nation denying.

By bringing Zionism back, and reminding the world of its true nature and foundations, Obama has done the prospects for peace the greatest service yet.

Al Monitor
April 9, 2013

WHAT DOES IT MEAN WHEN WE SAY 'THE JEWISH STATE'?

Nothing could be more harmful to the domestic debate within Israel and our ability to continue the project of Jewish sovereignty and wrestle with its implications than the phrase "Jewish and democratic."

Tzipi Livni, Israel's minister of justice, nominated on Aug. 19 professor Ruth Gavison in charge of drafting a constitutional law proposal that would enshrine Israel's status as the nation-state of the Jewish people, to address the slew of similar legislation initiatives. Her nomination and the phrasing of the laws as "Israel: Homeland of the Jewish people," inspire hope for repairing the damage in the national and international discourse caused by the phrase "Jewish and democratic."

The description of Israel as "Jewish and democratic" appears initially not in the Declaration of Independence – as is often thought – but in two 1992 constitutional laws pertaining to freedom of professions and dignity of all humans. Since that time, this has become the most common phrase describing the essence of Israel. But this formulation, originally intended to help resolve various tensions, has in itself become a source of problems. By its very phrasing as Jewish and democratic – joined together by the article "and" – the immediate assumption is that the two aspects are inherently contradictory and that Israel could hope for nothing more than a problematic compromise between the two.

Within Israel, as well as among Jews and Israel watchers, this equation has become one of antonyms – Jewish is the opposite of democratic. For those on the left, the democratic part of the equation has come to symbolize all the liberal and progressive values that they hold dear; and the Jewish side a mirror image of that. For the left, Jewish values are increasingly viewed as the repository of all that they detest. This is flipped for many on the right. For many on the right, Jewish values represent all that they care about and democracy the repository of all that threatens what they hold dear. Both left and right perceive Jewish and democratic as conflicting adjectives. They are wrong.

Democracy at its core is a system of governance. It is associated with specific values in the sense that liberal values are thought to be best expressed and ensured through the system of democracy, not because democracy is inherently liberal. An unchecked majoritarian democracy could be tyrannical and oppressive to minority rights, whereas a benevolent dictatorship could promote liberal values.

In seeking to understand Israel, the question then is not whether there is an inherent tension between Jewish and democratic, but whether there is an inherent tension between Jewish values and liberal values. The answer, of course, is: it depends.

The question is not whether there is an inherent tension between Jewish and democratic, but whether there is an inherent tension between Jewish values and liberal values. The answer, of course, is: it depends.

WINNING THE WAR OF WORDS

Like all ancient value systems that have been constantly evolving, Judaism can serve as a repository of liberal as well as ultra-conservative values. It is in the eye of the beholder and the interpreter. It is partial to neither of them. Jewish civilization, like all ancient civilizations, is so rich as to support any system of governance and any set of values that its bearers choose. Just as Confucianism can underpin a communist dictatorship and a capitalist state, so can Judaism underpin liberal democracy, a socialist utopia and authoritarian theocracy.

If anything, the sad reality is that many of those both on the left and right of Israel have forgotten how to argue for liberal values from within Jewish traditions and texts. The secular left has gone overboard in its desire to create a "new Jew" and, by and large, has given up on drawing on Jewish sources to argue for the liberal values that it holds dear. The left argues for progressive values almost exclusively from within foreign traditions. The religious right, for its side, has chosen to mine Jewish sources for limited political purposes and give up on a broader discussion of values in our society.

It is in Israel's Declaration of Independence, in which the word "democratic" does not appear, that the new state's aspirational values were best presented stating that "it will be based on freedom, justice and peace as envisaged by the prophets of Israel; it will ensure complete equality of social and political rights to all its inhabitants irrespective of religion, race or sex; it will guarantee freedom of religion, conscience, language, education and culture." These were the values chosen for the state, considered not only desirable but grounded in Jewish tradition.

Israel is the democratic state of the Jewish people, and it is our only sovereign state. It was established to be the homeland of the Jewish people and would not have come into being otherwise. It is democratic by necessity, and it is liberal by choice.

Liberal democracy is not inimical to paradoxes, ambiguities, contradictions and the constant tensions of human life and society, and is not designed to somehow make them go away. If anything, it is a response to them and is expressed through the continuous negotiation of its various paradoxes, ambiguities, contradictions and tensions. There is no inherent contradiction between "Jewish" and "democratic" or between "Jewish" and "liberal." The only question is how those living in the democratic state of the Jewish people – Jews and non-Jews alike – choose to interpret Jewish tradition, in all its variety and wealth, to organize their common lives in the present.

Al Monitor
September 4, 2013

ISRAEL AT SIXTY: NOT FOR THE FAINT OF HEART OR LAZY OF MIND

As it nears its 60th birthday, there is no use denying; Israel is not for the fainthearted. Whether you were born and raised here, chose to make *aliyah*, or spent your life engaging with Israel and its people, you know that at no point did Israel promise to make it easy for you, and at no point did you have cause to complain that it has been so.

Much like a high-maintenance girlfriend, Israel's draw is addictive, exciting and eternally frustrating. In return for never-ending efforts to woo her, not a trace of gratitude is to be offered – barely an appreciative smile. The frustrated lover might try to call it quits once and again, but her pull is too strong to resist. The drama of living with her is too addictive. Whether one is with her or away from her, she is not to be ignored.

Indeed, I suspect that most Israelis and those who carry Israel in their hearts are secretly addicted to drama. I know I am. The first criticism most Israelis are likely to level at any country that offers the specter of a quiet prosperous life amid lush greenery and perfect weather is "boring." It is an addiction bordering on bi-polarity, with Israelis exacting peculiar pleasure from the extreme oscillation between intense periods of (mostly unjustified) euphoria and extended swaths of wallowing in (also mostly unjustified) depression.

Life in Israel is one of constant negotiations between extremes. Israel fiercely insists on a national identity as a homeland for the Jewish people, at a time when many people around the world, mostly young, find nationalism a quaint and passé notion; it is a democratic circus in the center ring of the world's least democratic region. It is a highly developed country bordering on some of the world's least developed countries and regions. Yet, given the decibels of internal criticism most Israelis would find it hard to believe that Israel is ranked 23 among the world's countries on the UN's Human Development Index, (a standard means of measuring well-being, especially child welfare).

I suspect that most Israelis and those who carry Israel in their hearts are secretly addicted to drama. I know I am.

Israelis are very much in love with the world and could hardly sustain the thought of their national airport being closed, but are also absolutely certain that the world is against them and their little country. Israelis cannot wait to escape Israel, only to conclude that there's no place like home.

In the extremities of its being, Israel and life in Israel epitomize the reality of the human condition – that which most humans choose to ignore, but which is the fountain of all creation: that human life is fragile and that each new day brings with it the potential to transform our life as we know it. Israel is a place where people, young and old, dream, create, innovate, and initiate, while never forgetting, and always fearing, that all that has been built and accomplished might one day disappear in smoke. In Israel the notion that man makes plans and God laughs is an everyday reality (even if it is our God…).

Israel is not for the intellectually slothful either. It does not lend itself to neat categorizations. Its very existence forces one to re-examine established conventions and add nuances to rigid thought patterns. The society is fiercely secular, but also deeply Jewish. Israel is not a theocracy, but the Orthodox religious establishment has an official role in the life of its citizens. There are many citizens who view themselves as left-wing Zionists, but being Zionists would rule them out as left wing almost anywhere outside of Israel. The question of what it means to be the homeland of the Jewish people is one that is permanently relevant and ever changing. It challenges the mind and presents true dilemmas daily. Living in and with Israel means constant engagement with difficult problems with no simple, good or easy answers.

A. B. Yehoshua was right that life in Israel means nearly total engagement with Jewish dilemmas, but he is wrong if he thinks that engaging in these issues comes only from living in Israel and open only to Israelis. If anything, the ability to tackle some of the most difficult questions of life in Israel would only productively take place in the context of the entire Jewish people.

Israel was designed and created for the Jewish people by the Jewish people. Sixty years after its founding, this has not changed. Israel's very nature cannot be disconnected from that first element of its birth. To be the country of the Jewish people means much more than taking Jewish money. To be the country for the Jewish people means much more than being a shelter and destination of *aliyah*. With the Jewish people passing a critical threshold that has not been passed in more than 2500 years, in which the world's largest Jewish community resides in Israel, it is time for a new and restructured relationship between Israel and the Jewish people, one in which Israel gives as well as takes.

The future of the Jewish people depends now more than ever on Israel embracing its role as a source of leadership in Jewish issues. It is a role that requires investing resources in strengthening the Jewish people as a whole, not as some kind of "reserves in waiting" for *aliyah*, but in recognition of the inherent value for all Jews of the diversity of Jewish life. It is about calling upon the Jewish people to make Israel if not their first, their second home – not necessarily a physical one – but a home nonetheless. Israel should issue an invitation to all Jews everywhere to find their path to a life of engagement with Israel: intellectual, physical, emotional, full-time, part-time, or just once in a while.

Israel is a place where people, young and old, dream, create, innovate, and initiate, while never forgetting, and always fearing, that all that has been built and accomplished might one day disappear in smoke.

For too long, Israelis, and Israeli officials especially, "trained" Jews outside of Israel to "pay up and shut up," to put it harshly. I have heard too many Jews proudly proclaim that they support Israel financially and personally, but because they don't live in Israel they have nothing to say critically about it (mind you, this is not because they really have nothing to say). I find this attitude a bit too convenient for all involved. The Israeli side does not have to listen and the non-Israeli Jewish side does not have to think. But Israel desperately needs people who are willing to think long and hard about what it means to be the homeland of the Jewish people, express these thoughts and act to realize them. It was always difficult to square the circle of Israel's unique nature. It is far more difficult to do so at an age when a national homeland for the Jews appears intellectually out of sync with a new age. Smart, nuanced, sophisticated and visionary thinkers, wherever they may live, are still very much in demand.

Israel is no longer the precocious and promising *wünderkind* of its first 19 years. It is also no longer the cool "Don't f... with the Jews" (to quote *Munich*'s Daniel Craig), older brother of the 1960s and 1970s of clear-cut military victories and heroic operations. It is even perhaps no longer the promising beacon of change for the new and improved Middle East of the 1990s. Israel at sixty embraces its idiosyncrasy.

After decades of fruitless efforts to "be like everybody else," Israel is a country that is slowly coming to terms with its abnormality and embracing it. Normality is to be gotten elsewhere. Living in and with Israel no longer offers the razzle-dazzle of youth or the virility of early adulthood, but it offers the pleasures of maturity. Engaging with Israel today means being involved in a relationship that is substantial, fascinating and always unique.

Jewish Agency for Israel
Spring 2008

WINNING THE WAR OF WORDS

AN ISRAEL INTELLECTUAL DEFENSE FORCE

Israel is a state that, with all its economic and cultural achievements, continues to struggle for survival in a region that is hostile towards its very existence. The very notion that the Jewish people, as a people, have the right to self-determination and a state of their own in the only region in which they were ever sovereign, was opposed from the outset. Israel's ability to survive and even thrive amidst the surrounding hostility has been the result of its ability to identify the threats to its survival and to respond to them decisively.

Immediately upon its establishment – within hours of its declaration of Independence – Israel was threatened militarily. The mobilized armies of seven Arab armies were to be the means of its physical destruction. Fighter planes, tanks, guns and soldiers were mobilized again and again in an effort to rid the region of a Jewish state in its midst. And Israel, through the sacrifice of many of its best young men and women, repelled them again and again. Israel responded to the existential threat posed by Arab armies by building one of the world's mightiest military machines. War after war, attack after attack, Israel managed to demonstrate to the hostile armies around it that it would not be defeated by force. Twenty-five years after Arab armies first mobilized against Israel, the bloody and terrible 1973 Yom Kippur War was to be Israel's last conventional war. Within the course of a generation, Israel won the military battle for survival.

EINAT WILF

Just as we have the IDF, the Israel Defense Forces, we should now have the IIDF, the Israel Intellectual Defense Forces, committed to the intellectual defense of Israel.

For its enemies, armies would not be the means of Israel's destruction. But Israel's enemies did not give up on their goal – they merely changed the arena where their wars were fought. Beginning in the 1970s, international and domestic terrorism, as well as a petro-dollar driven Arab boycott, were the new tools of attack. The people of Israel were to be terrorized and economically strangled to submission. In response, Israel developed substantial skills in combatting terrorism – both international and domestic – and developed one of the world's most innovative export-based economies. Contrary to most countries in the world, Israel's economy does not depend on the region and survives as a virtual island. Victory was not immediate, but by the end of the 1990s the Arab boycott failed and was dissolved, and Israel's economy surpassed even those of the oil-rich states of the region. In the past decade, international and domestic terrorism were also put at bay, and even though attempts at attacks continue, terrorism no longer represents a strategic threat to Israel and its citizens are not terrorized.

But, as in the previous rounds, Israel's decisive victories in one arena merely forced its enemies to search new arenas where Israel is vulnerable. The new arena is one of ideas and images. In a bizarre return to square one, Israel is currently being attacked for its foundational idea. It is an attack on the idea that the Jewish people, as a people, have the right to self-determination and their own state in the only land in which they were ever sovereign – an idea without which there would be no Israel. Each one of the elements of this idea is under attack: the existence of the Jewish people as a people, rather than just a religion, is being questioned and dismissed. The idea that the Jewish people should therefore have the right to self-determination and a state of their own is rejected. The historic relationship between the Jewish people and the Land of Israel is also being denied. This attack on the ideas that underpin Israel – the attack on its very legitimacy as a state – is taking place in a variety of forums, from international forums such as the UN and its various bodies, to courts, to academia, to the media, the NGO world and social networks. And so, with the failure of physical attacks, an intellectual attack is being mounted. While this attack does not appear at first to be as dangerous and lethal as the others, it is no less threatening as it is targeting the very thing that makes Israel strong – its unique foundational idea.

Israel's ability to survive and thrive depends again on providing a strong, smart and definitive response to this attack. First, the importance, severity and nature of the threat must be acknowledged. While several years ago calls to head this issue seriously were dismissed by some as "fluff" compared with "serious" physical threats, the leadership of Israel and the Jewish world is now firmly behind this issue. Second, the same kinds of resources and structures that were mobilized in previous wars and battles should be put to work in this case. Just as we have the IDF, the Israel Defense Forces, we should now have the IIDF, the Israel Intellectual Defense Forces, committed to the intellectual defense of Israel. These structures should also reflect the nature of the threat and the arena – diverse and dispersed. Rather than hierarchical closed structures, we should have global, open and dispersed ones that allow for anyone who wants to serve in Israel's defense – whether they are members of parliament who believe in Israel's foundational idea, international legal luminaries, or 15-year-old kids with creative minds and laptops – to contribute to the effort.

For too long Israel has merely responded to attacks, but there is no reason why Israel should not mount its own campaigns.

Third, a battle doctrine should be developed that includes several key principles such as: don't just engage in defense – go on the offensive. For too long Israel has merely responded to attacks, but there is no reason why Israel should not mount its own campaigns. The absurdity of Israel being repeatedly attacked on human rights issues by some of the world's greatest offenders should not go unchallenged. Another principle should be to leave no arena unattended and to allow no lie to fester. Even the most ridiculous charges and the most obscure places need to be countered. Fourth, we should remember that the world does not consist only of European courts and west coast university campuses. Most of the world lives in the east. China and India are rising to world prominence. They do not have a complicated history with the Jewish people. On the contrary, there is tremendous sympathy for the Jewish people and the story of Israel. These are the places where we need to invest the most in building relationships and support for the future.

Finally, some of the traditional key messages need to be changed. Israel should not try to compete on victimhood. Any effort by Israel to show the world that we are greater victims than the others and that we suffer more is bound to fail. As a proud Zionist, I do not want to win in the competition of who is the greater victim. We did not build an independent state in order to arouse pity and wallow in misery. Our message should be one of responsibility. This is our strength and this is where we can challenge the other side – on their actions, decisions and responsibility for the historical outcomes.

While victory in this battle, as in others, is not likely to be swift, with the proper resources, organization and determination, it is within reach. After all, if there is any battle that the Jewish people should be able to win, it is the battle of words.

Presentation to International Consultation of
Jewish Parliamentarians
June 2011

EINAT WILF

A ROVING AMBASSADOR FOR ISRAEL

A roving ambassador-at-large for Israel and Zionism: that has been my unofficial title for the past year, as I found myself spending most of my time thinking, writing, and speaking on behalf of Israel, Zionism, and the Jewish state, at home and abroad. The word *hasbara* – in Hebrew, the act of explaining – is used to denote the work of advocacy for Israel. This word is often denigrated by outsiders, as well as many insiders. Israel's official advocates are pathetic, they say, to think that the cause of Israel's image problem is a lack of clear explanation.

But, if the past year has taught me anything, it is that some fundamental concepts need exactly what people are mocking: explanations. Whether it is 'Zionism', 'the Jewish People' or 'the Jewish State', these concepts are poorly understood and, often, badly misunderstood. So, to all the naysayers, I reply: unfortunately, there is no other way to address these misunderstandings than to explain, providing a broad overview of what these words meant in the past, what they mean today, and to whom.

The work of *hasbara*, of public diplomacy and advocacy, is also frequently imagined as high-flying live television debates when (hopefully) the eloquent Israeli sticks it to the anti-Israel speaker of the moment. However, *hasbara* goes far beyond this. Truly effective and long-lasting *hasbara* is about explaining the ideas and circumstances that formed the foundation of Israel's existence. And there is a growing audience for this. It only seems that we live in an ADHD world of sound bites, of crude black and white 'analysis', of simplistic notions of good and evil. Actually, I find that people want so much more than that. They want to understand, to appreciate complexity, to really 'get it'. I've been meeting these kinds of people in Israel in recent years. They come on delegations organised by a wide variety of groups, and it is these delegations – when thoughtfully designed and expertly carried out – that are perhaps the best tool for getting people to think in more nuanced and complex ways about Israel.

When people come to Israel, they realise there is a gap between the image and the reality. Only then are they are open to revisiting their assumptions and eager to really get to grips with Israel, Zionism, and the Jewish people.

The reason why delegations work so well is that in the case of Israel, the product is still far better than the image. Some would suggest that this says more about the image than the product, but the fact remains that almost all the people I've met are deeply and positively surprised by the reality of Israel – they are struck by its vibrancy, diversity, dynamism and openness. And while many come expecting a searing cauldron of explosive religious and ethnic violence, they are surprised by the sense of security and calm they experience once on its streets.

In short, when people come to Israel, they realise there is a gap between the image and the reality. Only then are they are open to revisiting their assumptions and eager to really get to grips with Israel, Zionism and the Jewish people. Once here, they are willing to devote hours, even days, to better understanding these concepts, the issues that shape Israel and the challenges it faces.

I meet many of these delegations – and many more of them have been coming to Israel in recent years – and it is always a pleasure to see the sheer diversity: from Canadians to Indians to Chinese; from African-American church leaders to atheist Scandinavians; from cynical British journalists to enthusiastic Hollywood producers; from members of parliament to those hoping to replace them; from global students of international relations to Jewish activists, and more. And I have come to see that when it comes to discussing Zionism, Judaism and the concept of the Jewish state, each group reads these foundational concepts through the lens of *their own* national, cultural and historical context.

It only seems that we live in an ADHD world of sound bites, of crude black and white 'analysis', of simplistic notions of good and evil. Actually, I find that people want so much more than that. They want to understand, to appreciate complexity, to really 'get it'.

For example, I was recently fascinated to encounter a delegation of Indian businessmen deeply disturbed by the implications of Zionism for India; telling me that in India, if every people with a shared history, language and culture dating back centuries were to want their own state, India would disintegrate into 500 different countries. They broadly accepted the idea of national self-determination (as it was certainly critical to their own modern liberation), but somehow the implications of Zionism – perhaps because it rested on such ancient connections, or perhaps because it only applied to only a few million people – were greater to them. Chinese academics, on the other hand, were comfortable with the idea of Judaism as an ancient civilisation and the unity of a people, a country, a language and a culture that is Israel, as well as with the goal of Zionism. To them, Judaism made much more sense as a civilisation than when it was reduced to a religion. Scandinavian atheists who thought that the Jewish state was strictly a religious idea were visibly relieved to learn that Zionism was, at its founding, a secular and even atheist endeavour, to which there are still many heirs in Israel. Yet African-American church leaders felt that my service to the Jewish people and the Jewish state meant that, at the core, I was a woman of God.

Ultimately, through all the diversity emerges a theme: commonality. Today, *all* peoples and *all* groups are struggling with questions of history, culture, religion, land, country, sovereignty, solidarity, identity and morality in the context of globalised modernity. Moreover, it is evident that none have found 'the answer'. Once the comfortable surface is scratched, no person and no peoples are truly at ease with all these dilemmas and struggles. In this context, the story of Zionism, unique and special, becomes part of a global mosaic of peoples struggling to make sense of this world, to find a place within it to call their own, a place they can feel at once a part and of the whole – a universal experience. It is when we engage in dialogue that we can understand this commonality and universality. Done well, it is the indispensable work of *hasbara* to help all peoples to see this commonality plainly.

Fathom
Spring 2014

WINNING THE MEDIA WAR

This summer, all of Israel's ambassadors, official and not, stationed and roving, moved from 'regular defense' to emergency mode. While the soldiers of the Israel Defense Forces (IDF) were fighting by air, ground and sea to defend Israel's citizens from threats from above and below, the self-enlisted soldiers in Israel's Intellectual Defense Forces, of whom I am one, mobilised on the airwaves, press and social media to stand up for Israel and Zionism. My uniform consisted mostly of a standard navy blue suit. I faced no danger while in the studios (unless the siren for 'Color Red' went off, as it frequently did). But the stakes were high; winning this 'other' war of words, images and ideas was no less important than winning the military campaign. The Prime Minister himself defined it as one of four fronts: military, home, media and legal.

As I made my way through the television studios – tough interviews at the BBC and Sky News, truly hostile ones at Al Jazeera and Russia Today – I felt that everything counted, from the suit I wore to the facial expressions I made. I was not just an expert but an Israeli and everything I said reflected not just on me but on my country. But there was no time to explain Israel's situation. The in-depth talks I had given to engage audiences all over the world about the story of Zionism and the meaning of Israel's existence were just not possible. In wartime it all became black and white; complexity was out and nuance was absent. There was no history, no context, and no real conversation; only images devoid of context, words devoid of meaning, allegations devoid of proof, and ancient libels revived.

There is no such thing as 'fighting fair' in this war of words and images. Experience has taught me that expressing empathy for the other, accepting responsibility for mistakes on our side, and acknowledging legitimate concerns by the other side, is abused to paint Israel in the darkest colours of evil. The word 'sorry' will be used to admit culpability; the word 'mistake' to convey evil intentions; the words 'we are not sure' to mean that we are sure of the opposite.

As much as we often feel beleaguered and demonised, I have no doubt that this is a war we will ultimately win, for two simple reasons: the story of a people picking themselves out of misery to assume responsibility for shaping their own fate is the far better story – and we have no other choice.

Hamas had a sinister strategy for their military and media campaigns. For the violent war in which our soldiers were fighting, Hamas placed rockets in their civilian areas and built tunnels into our civilian areas. In the media war, Hamas terrorised journalists reporting from their midst in order to censor every image of militants, every picture of rocket launchers stationed in playgrounds, and every video of a rocket being launched from a school. All that got out of Gaza were images that suggested Israel was carrying out motiveless attacks on women and children. The ancient blood libels at least put forward a reason for the Jews killing Gentile children; they needed to use their blood to bake their weird bread for their weird holiday. The new blood libel simply portrays Jews as 'baby killers' because that is what Jews do.

Speaking for Israel in times of war requires simple truths, stated clearly and often. Those who insist on holding on to their nuances in times of emergency need not apply. Stating the obvious is necessary: Israel has the right to protect itself. The people of Israel are defending themselves against indiscriminate attacks. Hamas is fighting to destroy the Jewish State and has no interest in living in peace side-by-side with Israel. Israel fights to save the lives of its citizens. Hamas fights by jeopardising the lives of citizens, theirs and ours. Israel takes unprecedented measures to avoid civilian casualties on both sides.

The military campaign is now at bay. The home front is calm. The legal front is warming up. The war of images and ideas continues, but the mode is now set to 'ongoing defense'. This is a long war in which victory will go to those who do not waver, who stand firm, and ultimately to those who have the better story. As much as we often feel beleaguered and demonised, I have no doubt that this is a war we will ultimately win, for two simple reasons: the story of a people picking themselves out of misery to assume responsibility for shaping their own fate is the far better story – and we have no other choice.

Fathom
Autumn 2014

Chapter 5

ON OTHER MATTERS: ELECTIONS, EDUCATION, AND ENTITLEMENT

"There are few 'conventional wisdoms' so widely accepted in Israel than the notion that 'our electoral system is broken and must be fixed.' In a society known for its contentiousness and inability to agree on almost anything, one must appreciate the mere fact of having such broad agreement on a central issue. Yet, in my experience, broad consensus does not necessarily imply wise policy."

"It's NOT the Electoral System, Stupid"
May 2015

"Every committee proposes a major overhaul. That's fine. But first – let's make sure that the class is calm, that mountains of garbage do not block the path to the classroom, that a class starts on time, that students actually attend class, that more than three students do the reading, that students are able to speak up in class without suffering insults from their peers, and that eggs are not hurled at teachers on their way to class."

"Back to Basics: How to Fix the Israeli Education System (at No Additional Cost)"
April 2008

"I had fallen prey to the belief that brains, talent, and hard work would naturally lead me to occupy the roles and places that I thought I merited. I believed that once I had completed my duties to the gods of merit – good grades, good schools, hard work – they would roll out the red carpet for me.….It took me five years to snap out of it."

Huffington Post
March 26, 2014

IT'S NOT THE ELECTORAL SYSTEM, STUPID

There are few "conventional wisdoms" so widely accepted in Israel as the notion that "our electoral system is broken and must be fixed." In a society known for its contentiousness and inability to agree on almost anything, one must appreciate the mere fact of having such broad agreement on a central issue. Yet, in my experience, broad consensus does not necessarily imply wise policy. And since a lively debate between well thought out positions is critical for the hammering out of better policies, I have decided to write this book. If this book serves to disturb the comfortable consensus, which has become the political rallying cry of so many Israelis both inside and outside the political system, it will have served the health of our public discourse and contribute to fact-based, and therefore better, policy making.

At the outset, let me be clear: the Israeli system is certainly imperfect. But I believe that every other possible alternative system has its own inventory of imperfections, which are mostly unfamiliar to us but just as bad as ours. As Alexander Hamilton wisely observed during the debate over the ratification of the now iconic American Constitution, the demand for perfection is a recipe for societal chaos.

The first time I began to suspect that the accepted conventional wisdom about the dysfunctionality of the Israeli system might not be so conventional – or might not even be so wise – was during my years of working as a foreign policy advisor to then Deputy Prime Minister Shimon Peres, today the President of Israel. Shimon Peres' schedule was routinely filled with meetings with heads of states, senior officials and influential politicians. The conversations ran the full gamut of geopolitical issues, with Peres' counterparts always taking pleasure in his sharp analysis of the geopolitics of the time and his visionary views.

As Alexander Hamilton wisely observed during the debate over the ratification of the now iconic American Constitution, the demand for perfection is a recipe for societal chaos.

It was only with respect to one issue that Shimon Peres failed to arouse the sympathy of his listeners – and that is when he would break into a bitter complaint about the inadequacies of the Israeli electoral system and the impossible limitations it places on those who operate within it. Of course, one must always be wary when a man who has enjoyed such a long and fruitful political career (73 years and counting!) and has been able to accomplish so much for his country, complains about the limitations of the political system. One would better assume that the extent of these complaints is but the flipside of the extent of his vision, which any system, by definition, is bound to limit (in that he is indeed the heir to Ben-Gurion, who also complained bitterly about the system that allowed him to do and achieve so much for his people).

However, it was not this discrepancy that agitated his counterparts during that part of the discussions – rather,

WINNING THE WAR OF WORDS

it was their impatience to break in with their own litany of complaints about the failings of their own political systems. I recall one meeting with a senior French politician, chairperson of one of France's major parties, who at the time of complaint did not know that, like Shimon Peres, he was to become president of his country. As soon as Shimon Peres completed detailing what he saw as the unbearable faults of the Israeli system ("Imagine your having to try to get anything done with 12 parties in parliament, it's impossible!"), his French counterpart began to rail against the failings of the French one ("Nothing ever gets done in France without a revolution! The only way we are ever able to accomplish anything is by placing guillotines in our town squares"). Like two sick people waiting in line for the doctor listing their various ailments, they had no sympathy for the other's sufferings. Both were deeply convinced that their own particular illness was uniquely disturbing and far more serious than the idle complaints of the other.

Another fascinating encounter took place with yet another man who would be president, but who was then a promising young Senator from Chicago. After a wide-ranging conversation in which the Senator sat absorbed, Shimon Peres proceeded to detail the failings of the Israeli system with its 12 parties. Barack Obama listened coolly and responded calmly, "Oh, but we have 12 parties too – they just all happen to be within the Democratic Party..." These exchanges repeated themselves like variations on a theme country after country, politician after politician. Reading about the disgust many

British had for their own electoral system after the 2010 parliamentary elections, I have concluded that there is not an electorate in the world that is really satisfied with its electoral system. I have also noted with bemusement that all those who complained seem to go on to become presidents of their countries, raising the possibility that these complaints served perhaps as a way to ward off the political evil eye.

I had to ask myself: could it be that the Israeli system is not as bad as we believe it to be? And if it is as bad, could it at least be no worse than others? Or to paraphrase Churchill's *bon mot* about democracy: could it be that Israel's electoral system is the worst in the world, except for all the others? I decided to look into the matter, to go beyond the typical arguments and scrutinize some of the more fundamental issues.

First off, I decided to go beyond the surface to check the fundamentals. I asked how many countries have been continuously democratic since 1948, when Israel was established. By democratic, I mean in the full sense of a free, liberal democracy rather than a sham majoritarian one, and by continuously democratic, I mean no spells of dictatorships or military rule, no civil wars, and no suspended or overruled elections – that is to say, without serious breaches, disturbances or radical changes to the system; the things we should truly care about when we think of the stability of our electoral systems. It turns out that there are only 21 to 23 such countries in the world. Israel is one of them. They include: Austria, Australia, Belgium, Canada, Costa

Rica, Denmark, Finland, Germany, Iceland, Ireland, Israel, Italy, Japan, Luxembourg, the Netherlands, New Zealand, Norway, Sweden, Switzerland, the United Kingdom and the United States. India, the world's largest democracy, is a borderline case given the 21-month state of emergency that Indira Gandhi had President Fakhruddin Ali Ahmed impose on India between 1975-1977, in which she ruled by decree and suspended elections and civil liberties. France, the universal icon of republicanism, is also a borderline case because the collapse of the 4th Republic in 1958 and the establishment of the 5th Republic indicates a lack of continuity. But, since France and India on the whole have been fairly continuous constitutional democracies, they are included.

Twelve of these 23 countries have an electoral system similar to Israel's, namely: proportional election by party list, and multiple parties in a parliamentary system. These twelve include: Austria, Belgium, Costa Rica, Denmark, Finland, Iceland, India, Israel, Luxembourg, Sweden, Norway, Switzerland and the Netherlands. But for the absence of a minimum electoral threshold for parties, the Dutch system is almost identical to that of Israel: proportional election by party list in a single electoral region and multiple parties in a parliamentary system.

I had to ask myself: could it be that the Israeli system is not as bad as we believe it to be? And if it is bad, could it at least be no worse than others?

Four other countries have variations of the proportional system. Germany, Italy, and New Zealand have the *Mixed Member Proportional Representation System*. This is a variant of the proportional system. The overall total of party members in the elected body is, like the proportional system, intended to mirror the overall proportion of votes received. It differs from the classic proportional system because it includes a set of members elected by geographic constituency who are deducted from the party totals so as to still maintain overall proportionality. Ireland has the *Single Transferable Vote System*. This is a system designed to achieve proportional representation through preferential voting, which is a ballot structure in which voters rank candidates in order of relative preference. Ireland's system, therefore, is even more highly proportional than Israel's. So, of the 23 continuously democratic countries, 17 have some form of proportional voting and only three – Britain, Canada and the United States – have a 'first past the post' regional system. Japan, France and Australia have their own idiosyncratic systems which, in the case of Japan and Australia, also have a proportional component. Only two of the 23 countries have a clear presidential system: the United States and Costa Rica; and Costa Rica is also the only country in the world that combines the presidential with a proportional party list electoral system like Israel's. France's system includes strong presidential elements, and could be considered a mid-level, hybrid system between a presidential and a parliamentary system (reflecting the twin forces of modern French history of republicanism and monarchy).

WINNING THE WAR OF WORDS

That Israel is even included in this "Club of 23" is extraordinary. Israel achieved democratic maturity and created a democratic tradition faster than any other society in human history and did so during a war of independence in which it was fighting for its very existence. It absorbed millions of immigrants, most of whom came from countries with no democratic traditions. It created a functioning parliamentary system with serious working committees and, despite its often boisterous behavior, a functioning parliamentary etiquette in which even enemies of the very idea of a Jewish State have freedom of speech and often preside as acting Speakers of the House over Knesset deliberations. It is also the only former colony, mandate or protectorate (with the exception of India) ruled by an imperial power included in the "Club of 23." Furthermore, it is the only democratic country in history that has been in a *formal* state of war, with all the constitutional dilemmas this implies, since its founding. If anything, Israel's democratic and constitutional evolution is one of the most extraordinary achievements in the political history of the human race.

The founding of the United States as a constitutional democracy is often called the "miracle at Philadelphia," yet the American founding fathers were products of three preparatory traditions: the British constitutional tradition going back to the Magna Carta (1215), through to the Petition of Right (1628) and the English Bill of Rights (1689); the European Enlightenment tradition with its stress on the freedom and dignity of the individual as well as religious tolerance; and the colonial tradition of self-government. Historians have termed the thirteen colonies: "Thirteen schools of self-government." All thirteen had been de facto, self-governing, constitutional republics for decades before the War of Independence. By 1776, Virginia and Massachusetts, the two major players in the revolution against Britain, had been self-governing for a longer period of time than has elapsed from the American Civil War to today. The youngest colony, Georgia, had been self-governing for a longer period of time than half the present member countries of the United Nations. From this, we see that the founding fathers of the United States were the most prepared group in history for the experiment in democratic self-government.

The real miracle is the "miracle in Tel Aviv": A group of men and women from such outposts of political enlightenment and democratic tradition as Pinsk, Warsaw, Moscow, Sana'a, and Baghdad created a robust constitutional democracy with more systemic stability than that great revolutionary icon, France, three years after the Holocaust and surrounded by millions of fanatics threatening to exterminate them. Moreover, this has not been a static stability; it has been a vigorous evolving stability with constantly expanding constitutional protections and cultural broadmindedness. While there is still structural discrimination and cultural prejudice against minorities – as there is in every other country in the world, irrespective of electoral system – there is no official legal or constitutional discrimination and the progress of rights for Israel's Arab citizens has been constant and substantive; this despite Israel having been at war with the Arab world since its inception. Oriental Jewish music, cultural expression and food have moved from the margins into the mainstream. The status of women, while still lagging behind Scandinavia, is probably equal to the USA and is more than a match for France, Germany and Italy. Gay rights and cultural acceptance are amongst the most advanced in the world. For a system so "flawed," these are truly extraordinary achievements.

The real miracle is the "miracle in Tel Aviv": A group of men and women from such outposts of political enlightenment and democratic tradition as Pinsk, Warsaw, Moscow, Sana'a, and Baghdad created a robust constitutional democracy with more systemic stability than that great revolutionary icon, France, three years after the Holocaust and surrounded by millions of fanatics threatening to exterminate them.

Measured against these achievements, I pondered the possible reasons for the exaggerated claims made by the reformers regarding the benefits of the particular reforms they were proposing. I was reminded of some of the excellent courses I took at the INSEAD Business School in France about the various distortions of supposedly rational decision-making, including the "law of unintended consequences." Building on the work of Nobel Prize-winner Daniel Kahneman and his partner Amos Tversky (both Israelis), we explored the human tendency towards overconfidence. One memorable phrase of the professor remains with me: "The only people who are truly able to assess the odds they face in their various endeavors are the clinically depressed." The technical term for this is "optimism bias," which is the demonstrated systematic tendency for people to be overly optimistic about the outcome of planned actions. This is the kind of overconfidence that is painfully apparent in those who seek to reform the system and promise so much in return.

Optimism bias is also related to another classic tendency. Those who propose change often make an asymmetric comparison between the faults of the present situation, which are empirical and easy to observe, and the expected benefits of the post-change situation, which are completely speculative. Such individuals are typically blind to the benefits of the present situation, which are taken for granted, as well as the potential and as yet unknown faults of the future post-reform situation. Well-meaning reformers often find it impossible to imagine that their pet reform could engender as many problems as the existing one. It has been noted, with some amusement, that this failure of thinking leads to the high incidence of divorce, as most people fail to see the benefits of their married condition and imagine the wonderful life as free divorcees, until it is too late.

The asymmetry in comparison refers to the fact that for every aspect of the comprehensive current system, a more appealing alternative aspect is cherry picked from a variety of different systems by the reformers and then presented as "obviously" being superior. Electoral reformers almost never compare the entirety of the Israeli system to the entirety of systems in other countries. The flawed thinking in this method of comparison is that one could pick and choose from each system a single aspect while ignoring the complete political, economic and social ecosystem of a country.

For example, many reformers have the dignity and majesty of the British Parliament's decorum in the back of their minds when advocating change – especially when comparing it to the obvious rudeness and chaotic behavior of the Knesset. The fistfights and brawling in the Japanese and Italian Parliaments, among others, somehow escape their attention; the utter boredom of American Congressional debates somehow does not come to mind. The hours spent in dull discussions in a nearly empty parliament outside Britain's exciting question time are also conveniently forgotten.

Armed with my modest research on continuous democracies, remembering the lessons of my academic education and having experienced firsthand the frustration of politicians in numerous countries with their own systems, I began comparing electoral systems and measured the Israeli system against them. This turned into a bit of a hobby for me. And like all confirmed hobbyists, I have been avidly collecting facts, bits of information and anecdotes about electoral systems around the world. As my collection expanded, it became quite clear that seen from up close, very few systems, none in fact, hold up to the assumptions we make about them when seen from afar and outside. The more I learned, the more I became an entrenched electoral conservative, firmly and deeply opposed to fundamental changes in the Israeli electoral system. I had become committed to exposing the intellectual fallacies inherent in most of the arguments on the matter, and to unearthing the hidden dangers of radical reform that wide-eyed, overconfident reformers fail to notice or refuse to acknowledge. Israel's dreadful experience with the reformist arguments that led to the direct election of the prime minister is a perfect example of this.

In 1992, Israel adopted a system in which the voters directly elected the prime minister – meaning that the PM would be elected separately from the Knesset rather than be the first member on the party list of the Knesset party that formed the government. Its advocates claimed that this method would not only be more democratic – since it would more accurately reflect the will of the people regarding who should be prime minister – but that it would also produce more stable governments, since the power of the prime minister would be dependent on the will of the people rather than the whim of second rank politicians in his own and smaller parties. The theoretical reasoning and internal logic behind the proposal was solid and Israel became the only parliamentary democracy in the world to have this system. The Prime Minister was directly elected by the voters, separate from the Knesset, in 1996, 1999 and 2001. This experiment in electoral reform was abandoned in 2001 because it had resulted in even more instability and the electoral system returned to its former and present format, but with a residue of the greater instability that the reform had bequeathed to Israel's political culture.

The reform failed because it enabled voters to split their vote between parties and individuals, resulting in an even greater splintering of the party system. Formerly, the Prime Minister's party was the dominant core party which formed the basis of the government coalition, and would have anywhere from 40-50 seats. As a consequence of the direct election system, the PM's party had fewer than 30 seats; a pattern that continued in part for a decade after the reform was repealed. The government became more, rather than less, dependent on small parties and thus even less able to implement its policies. The smaller parties got bigger and the bigger parties got smaller. Inexperienced and irresponsible politicians gained greater clout. Given the sociology of politics, in which parties build constituencies that develop vested interests in the further success of their party, this splintered situation continues to this day, to the detriment of Israeli politics. This is an instructive warning for potential reformers who base their proposals on the rational theoretical rather than on the empirical political. As one should beware of Greeks bearing gifts, so should one be beware of academics bearing electoral reforms.

***Even in the matter of electoral reform, Tevye in* Fiddler on the Roof** *had it right all along – it's all about "tradition."*

Another defining moment in my conversion to electoral conservatism came after a meeting with the Dutch Ambassador in Israel. Enjoying a lovely lunch by the Tel-Aviv seaside, we discussed the always-engrossing matter of electoral reform. Holland is the country with the system that most closely resembles that of Israel (single district, parliamentary multiparty system, proportional, party list electoral system). The Ambassador told me that much like Israel, electoral reform had been a favorite cause with broad support in Holland for a very long time. Yet, after observing Israel's dramatic failure with electoral reform, the Dutch came to the following conclusion: when it comes to electoral systems, tradition matters. Proficiency in the "ins and outs" of one's political system is a fundamental prerequisite for political professionalism. Politics is a profession with its own skill sets and intellectual and temperamental requirements, and every electoral system requires its own idiosyncratic political expertise. Radical changes to the system would turn all its protagonists into amateurs and amateurism in politics is not a virtue. It does damage to constitutional, operational and democratic effectiveness.

Taking a cue from the Dutch Ambassador, I realized that the standard for discussion about electoral reform must be empirical; it must be in terms of other existing electoral systems. There is nothing that cannot be done with comparisons to speculative, nonexistent electoral systems or with hypothetical constructs that have an ironclad, internal, theoretical logic but no relation whatsoever to the empirical reality of political life. Observing Israel's unfortunate failure, the prudent Dutch realized that given what appears to be an equal chance of doing worse after reform as doing better, there is inherent value in electoral tradition. The Dutch realized that there is something important to be said for the fact that citizens, politicians and aspiring politicians know the terms and parameters of the system in which they are making their political choices, year after year, election after election. And so it is through the Dutch Ambassador that I realized that even in the matter of electoral reform, Tevye in *Fiddler on the Roof* had it right all along – it's all about "tradition."

Thomas Jefferson also recognized the value of political tradition when, in America's *Declaration of Independence,* he wrote that:

> Prudence, indeed, will dictate that Governments long established should not be changed for light and transient causes; and accordingly all experience hath shewn, that mankind are more disposed to suffer, while evils are sufferable, than to right themselves by abolishing the forms to which they are accustomed.

In other words, unless the government itself has collapsed or become illegitimate in the eyes of large numbers of the citizenry, it is always better to leave well enough alone; certainly not to change it "for light and transient causes." The British had become illegitimate in the eyes of many colonial residents; as did the French throne soon after in the eyes of the French. Both peoples were ready to fight and die to change the system. The Fifth Republic of France arose on the ruins of the collapsed Fourth Republic when the French State simply ceased to function. The situation in Israel is nowhere near approaching either extremity. Thus prudence "will dictate" that we suffer the known flaws of our system while trying to ameliorate them before we embark on a program of reform and installing the flaws of an unknown system because we are annoyed by "light and transient causes."

"It's NOT the Electoral System, Stupid"
Co-written with Tsvi Bisk
2014 (Hebrew)

BACK TO BASICS: HOW TO FIX THE ISRAELI EDUCATION SYSTEM (AT NO ADDITIONAL COST)

The education system is lying on the floor, bleeding, in need of first aid. It needs to get to an emergency room urgently. The bleeding must be stopped. This is not the time to tell the education system that it needs to adopt a healthier lifestyle and do more exercise. The education system cannot be sent to the emergency room and the gym simultaneously. The system is struggling to survive. It has to be nursed back to health before improving its life. It has to be made to function again.

It is nowhere more true that "the road to hell is paved with good intentions" than in the education system. The system is filled with numerous well-meaning people, probably more than in any other system. Teachers, parents, administrators, and many others all want better education. They all want to do the right thing. And all of them are united in their wish to see knowledgeable, social, law-abiding, well-mannered, socially committed, and public spirited students graduate the system. Why is this not happening? Why do we all share the feeling that when it comes to education we are on the express train to hell? Well, because the road to heaven is paved with hard, dull, and annoying work that seems to have little to do with the grand mission of education.

Anyone can point out the ailments of the education system: violence, lack of discipline, over-emphasis of grades at the expense of actual learning, and countless hours spent passively sitting in class. However, every committee that is set up to provide a solution seems to ignore these problems. Committee proposals typically discuss curriculum, budgetary, and structural changes. Currently, these are irrelevant. At most, implementing them will bring about marginal improvements. Nevertheless, they do not address real problems or provide real solutions.

It is nowhere more true that "the road to hell is paved with good intentions" than in the education system.

Every committee proposes a major overhaul. That's fine. But first – let's make sure that the class is calm, that mountains of garbage do not block the path to the classroom, that the class starts on time, that students actually attend class, that more than three students do the reading, that students are able to speak up in class without suffering insults from their peers, and that eggs are not hurled at teachers on their way to class. How can learning take place in a violent, stressful, hurtful, and ugly environment? The process of learning requires a secure and stress free environment. In the current system, teachers and students are subject to impossible pressures. One cannot teach and learn under such conditions. What is the purpose of proposing new assessment schemes, incentive plans, and curriculum changes under these conditions? Someone whose arms and legs are broken will not run a marathon even if offered a million dollar incentive. That person needs first aid. Billions of dollars have been invested in useless projects while a dysfunctional system that is in a state of war continues to hemorrhage. When the building's foundations are shaky, investing in quality Italian marble on the second floor is a waste of money. Ministers typically don't want to do "small" reforms. Who wants to deal with discipline in the schools? Who wants to spend their time monitoring that daily rules of conduct are being followed? The educational committee that would address the cleaning schedule in classrooms, the bothersome rings of mobile phones, the manner in which students enter and exit the classroom, and the threat-filled demands that are made to teachers to raise grades has not yet been created. These are supposedly "small" things that are not relevant to Education with a capital E. Ministers prefer to set up committees to propose grandiose overhauls of the system even if implementation is zero. The mere act of establishing a committee is considered action. Ministers, Director Generals, administrators, and committee members prefer to discuss structural and curricular changes and incentive schemes. It is always more fascinating, heroic, and grand to move around organizational boxes, set up new departments, require that results be measured and incentives aligned with results, as well as to debate the content of history, literature, and civics textbooks. These are important, valuable, and given the current challenges, completely irrelevant matters.

One could forgive the committees' proclivity to offer an energy drink to an injured patient, if it were not that the finger is usually pointed at the one part that prevents the system from complete collapse – the teachers. The teachers are the tourniquet that prevents the hemorrhaging from turning fatal. The continued willingness of teachers to stand at the front line and to keep fighting maintains a semblance of functionality. Given that the system has abandoned the teachers and systematically prevented them from doing their job properly, the fact that educational work still takes place is a miracle that is the result of private struggles by determined principals and teachers. The education system is at war, but the generals have escaped from the field and abandoned the soldiers at the front.

The hatred and contempt of teachers are undermining the system. It has now become "obvious" that the core problem is bad teachers. It's incorrect and not at all obvious.

Ministers and administrators cause serious damage when they seek to implement reforms "in spite of the teachers." Who, exactly, is going to implement the reforms? Who will educate? It should be the other way around. The question that should guide any effort at reform should be how to give teachers the most auspicious conditions in which to do their work. The system should mobilize to help the teachers teach and implement the required changes. The system depends on the teachers' ability to function properly.

The hatred and contempt of teachers is undermining the system. It has now become "obvious" that the core problem is bad teachers. This is incorrect and not at all obvious.

The problem is not the teachers. Not that there aren't bad teachers – there are. But the system paralyzes the good teachers, or those who could have been good given the minimal necessary conditions. Teachers go into classrooms and face students without backing and without tools. They are condemned to endlessly handling students and parents who seek to undermine their authority. These teachers, under different conditions and another system, would have realized their potential. It would then have become clear that their potential is significant.

The problem is not with individual teachers. It is systemic. Put a good person in a bad system and the system will usually win. The fantasy of replacing the existing teachers with some mythological teachers outside the system who are just waiting to get in is just that – a fantasy. The mythological teachers that we all seek are, in large part, already within the system. They need only be allowed to realize their potential.

Management and organizational studies and years of experience demonstrate that in almost all large organizations that employ large numbers of people, the personnel qualities are distributed 80:10:10 – 10 percent are superheroes, 10 percent are unfit for their job, and 80 percent are well meaning and capable of good work. A functional system takes that 80 percent and makes the most of it. A dysfunctional system takes that 80 percent and paralyzes it. This general principle is applicable to the education system that employs 130,000 people. Right now, the system paralyzes the vast majority of teachers. As a result, it seems that 90 percent of teachers are lousy, when in reality, such teachers constitute no more than 10 percent. The 80 percent of teachers who could have been good or even very good are unable to function in the current environment. Even the superheroes are faced with challenges that demand the full use of their superpowers.

The schools and teachers that are still able to function under the current conditions are the exception. A national public education system cannot rely on isolated local initiatives by principals and teachers. It cannot depend on the efforts of individuals that manage to succeed against all the odds. Today, all schools and teachers are engaged in some kind of effort to find creative solutions that would allow learning to take place in their schools and classrooms. Nevertheless, this will not save the system. To free the teachers and principals to do their work, they need to be freed of the need to find creative solutions to a chaotic situation. The solution – any solution – has to be systemic.

Teachers who are abused, disrespected, despised, isolated, and ignored in the process of formulating and making policy become paralyzed and paralyzing teachers.

The teachers are the key element in the system, and the conditions that allow them to function properly need to be created. Teachers who are abused, disrespected, despised, isolated, and ignored in the process of formulating and making policy become paralyzed and paralyzing teachers. Attempts to downplay the value of teachers contribute to the ongoing destruction.

WINNING THE WAR OF WORDS

This book was written after none of those who seek to improve education in Israel took the obvious first step or did the most basic act – ask the teachers what should be done. The quote by Professor Robert Stake that opens this book presents an idea that is almost obvious – the most experienced and best teachers are those who have the knowledge of what is needed to improve the education system. However, until now, no one has turned to the teachers to seek their advice. Not really. Committee after committee has ignored the teachers, their experience, and accumulated knowledge.

The vast distance between the personal success in the classroom of the best and most experienced teachers and the obtuseness of the system is irritating and exasperating. Students adore their best teachers, parents struggle to secure these teachers for their children, and the system continues as it always has: disrespecting and ignoring the teachers, and insisting on putting forth proposals that are irrelevant and will do nothing to prevent the continuing decline. For decades, teachers have had to hear irrelevant recommendations from disconnected committees and listen to useless lectures by people who have no clue what it takes to stand in a classroom, teach a class, captivate the students' attention, and educate them. Teachers have had to observe committees that come and go from the sidelines, knowing full well before anyone else why these committees would, despite their best intentions, fail to bring about the desired improvements. All this went on while they themselves knew what had to be done to save the system.

Superb teachers prove day in and day out that things could be different, that one need not consent to the mounting violence and increasing chaos. They know how to solve problems, but are pushed aside when policy makers fail to see what is under their own noses. The experienced and best teachers know that their successes are not the result of magical acts, nor are they dependent on their personality or charisma. The entire system could do what they do every day. This book was written to give a voice to teachers and to detail the experience and knowledge that has been accumulated by the best of them.

The book is divided into three parts that build upon each other. It opens with a discussion of the current situation and the required solutions, and ends with a vision for a school of the future.

The first part – the bulk of this book – deals with the emergency the system is currently experiencing. It begins with a description of the various problems, including the violence and lack of discipline that are paralyzing the schools. Many people outside the system refuse to believe the depth and breadth of the problems or the severity of the situation. While reading, many would prefer to believe that these descriptions reflect "other places." However, the emergency is nationwide, in every school and every classroom. With massive efforts, individual principals and teachers are able to achieve a relative calm, but there is no teacher who does not face these challenges.

WINNING THE WAR OF WORDS

This part calls for a declaration of an emergency throughout the education system and a total mobilization of the system – principals, teachers, parents, and students – to address it. Until the system gets out of this situation, this book calls for avoiding allocating any managerial resources to other matters – no new books, no new organizational boxes, and no new pay or incentive structures. All of these can wait for the next phase. Any effort to implement initiatives in these areas, given the shaky foundations of the system, is bound to fail.

After describing the situation, this part of the book details solutions for escaping the emergency. The recommendations are offered at three levels – policies that the ministry of education should lead, solutions that school principals could implement, and steps that teachers could enact in their own classrooms. Success depends on implementation at all levels. However, some recommendations are put forth in a manner that school principals and teachers could implement immediately, even if the ministry of education procrastinates. It is important to emphasize that the proposed solutions are not accompanied by any demand for additional budgets – only changed policy.

The second part of the book deals with improvements that could be introduced to schools after the emergency has passed. It is futile – and impossible – to implement the proposals in this part of the book before overcoming the emergency. This part is based on making better use of the most wasted resources of the education system: the students' talents and the teachers' experience. The talent of students is one of the most wasted resources in the system. This waste also has severe implications for the students' personal growth and their ability to reach maturity with a sense of worth and confidence.

This part also offers ways to improve the flow of information through the system and to make better use of the immense expertise that teachers accumulate in order to enable new teachers to start from a higher point and make more rapid progress. The recommendations in this part are designed to ensure that all teachers can function at the highest level and the system would actually reduce rather than increase the gaps between different teachers. The implementation of the recommendations in the second part does not require additional budgets either. Rather, it shows how to release the potential of highly valuable resources that currently go to waste. Implementing the recommendations in the first two parts of the book is bound to take the rickety carriage that is today's education system and turn it into a racing car.

The third and last part discusses the school of the future. It presumes that following the implementation of the first and second parts of the book, a new educational culture will be created that will allow for the establishment of new kinds of schools. It offers a vision for a new kind of school, adapted to the challenges of the current century. This part points to several ways in which the elements of this school of the future could be introduced in the existing system. This part is designed to leave us with a dream of the future and to ensure that once the rickety carriage has become a racing car, we will learn to fly.

Foreword from the book "Back to Basics: How to Fix the Israeli Education System (at No Additional Cost)"
April 2008 (Hebrew)

THE RED CARPET SYNDROME

"I'm really smart. I'm talented. I work hard. Heck, I'm graduating from Harvard. So what's keeping the Israeli Prime Minister's Office? They must have forgotten. Otherwise, they would have called to say, 'Hello, Ms. Wilf, we are thrilled that you are finally graduating from Harvard. There's been a terrible vacuum here for the past four years. How soon can you be here?'"

Those were my thoughts nearly twenty years ago as I prepared to embark on my life as a Harvard graduate. I had done my share and now it was time for the world to do its share. Wasn't that the contract? I excelled in my education. I worked hard. I strived to do better. I even graduated from the world's top university. In a world that promised to reward brains, talent, and hard work I was supposed to be home free. Someone, somewhere was responsible for carrying out the world's end of the bargain and hand me the roles and jobs that I craved. I had earned it. I was entitled to it. No?

No, I learned. The world tarried. No one called. No one knocked on my door. No message had come demanding my immediate presence at the helm. It took me five years of running spreadsheets in consulting and investing to realize that I had fallen victim to the malady that was contracted by so many of our youngest and brightest: The Red Carpet Syndrome.

The Red Carpet Syndrome is the sense of entitlement that comes not from wealth or lineage, but of merit. Yes, even merit can lead to entitlement.

WINNING THE WAR OF WORDS

I had fallen prey to the belief that brains, talent, and hard work would naturally lead me to occupy the roles and places that I thought I merited. I believed that once I had completed my duties to the gods of merit – good grades, good schools, hard work – they would roll out the red carpet for me. I would then walk it daintily, landing softly on the couch of my dream job. I would be asked to be Israel's ambassador to the United Nations and later, its foreign minister. Other than the fatal illusion that college in America resembles "Grease," it's probably the reason I went to Harvard in the first place. I wanted to make sure that when invitations were issued, I would be prepared with a top-notch education and a diplomat's English.

It took me five long years to snap out of it. And I am one of the lucky ones. Others are not so fortunate. So many spend a lifetime waiting for the red carpet to be rolled out. They wait for the phone call that never arrives, for the invitation that never comes, for the note that tells them that the world has taken notice and is now prepared to give them their due. Over time they become bitter adults. They stand by as they witness a bunch of bozos (in their view) assume the roles of Senators, Congressmen, Fortune 500 CEO's, movie stars, and best-selling authors. The more these "bozos" ascend, the more those plagued by the Red Carpet Syndrome retreat into their sense of having been the victims of a grave injustice. Like Esau, they feel they have been robbed of their rightful bequest.

The Red Carpet Syndrome is the sense of entitlement that comes not from wealth or lineage, but of merit. Yes, even merit can lead to entitlement.

Others wither slowly in jobs and careers they never chose, simply because those were the only places that rolled out the red carpet for them. I do not know a single teenager who dreams of becoming a consultant or investment banker. I doubt there is a single teenager who knows what consultants or investments bankers do. Yet, out of my graduating class of sixteen hundred at Harvard College, eight hundred had applied to consulting firms and investment banks. In a school that prides itself on diversity, this makes no sense, unless you are aware that consulting firms and investment banks are the only ones that do roll out the red carpet. They wine and dine the students. They tell them how great they are. The students only need to apply. And so, thousands of students from top universities across America seek jobs they never knew they wanted, only because they do not know how to get the ones they have always dreamed of. Decades later they wake up, withered inside, having spent a lifetime doing what they never wanted to do; their teenage dreams and ambitions all but a sad memory.

The lucky ones snap out of it. They learn that in this world, and in this life, no one invites anyone to anything. They realize that the jobs worth having, the roles worth playing, the places worth leading do not roll out the red carpet for anyone. These places don't know who you are and they don't care. There are no rules for success, no trodden paths to the top. Unless your goal in life is to become an upper middle class professional, nothing is guaranteed. Anything worth doing requires risk, misery, repeated failure (of the real kind, not the fake kind you write about in your college application essay), and humiliating self-promotion. You might even run the risk of regretting not having taken the safe path – but you will be alive.

So snap out of it. Forget the red carpet. There is but one rule for living your own life, and no one else's: If you want to attend the party, crash it. I did.

The Huffington Post
March 26, 2014

See also: Harvard Crimson
June 5, 2006

CPSIA information can be obtained
at www.ICGtesting.com
Printed in the USA
BVHW041818140420
577588BV00012B/421